THE IMPORTANCE OF TEACHING

A Memorandum
to the
New College Teacher

Report of the

Committee on Undergraduate Teaching
C. Easton Rothwell *Chairman*

The Committee on
Undergraduate Teaching

C. Easton Rothwell, *Chairman*
President-Emeritus of Mills College
Regional Consultant on Educational Development of The Asia Foundation
Harriet B. Creighton
Professor of Botany, Wellesley College
Maure L. Goldschmidt
Professor of Political Science, Reed College
James L. Jarrett, *Executive Director*
Associate Dean, School of Education, University of California
Morris T. Keeton
Dean of the Faculty and Professor of Philosophy, Antioch College
Alvin B. Kernan
Associate Provost and Professor of English, Yale University
Wilburt J. McKeachie
Chairman of Psychology Department, University of Michigan
John U. Munro
Director of Freshman Studies, Miles College, formerly Dean, Harvard College, Harvard University
George N. Shuster
Assistant to the President, University of Notre Dame
John M. Thompson
Professor of History, Indiana University
Kenneth W. Thompson
Vice-President, The Rockefeller Foundation
Pauline Tompkins
President, Cedar Crest College
John Useem
Professor of Sociology, Michigan State University
Paul L. Ward
Executive Secretary, American Historical Association
W. Max Wise
Professor of Higher Education, Teachers College, Columbia University

Contents

Foreword

The Committee on Undergraduate Teaching was formed in 1964 in response to an obvious and urgent need to improve college teaching and to give it greater importance. Almost as obvious was the opportunity to achieve both better teaching and more emphasis upon it in the colleges and universities.

The Committee received its mandate from The Hazen Foundation, which also provided the funds that made possible its work. The Committee functioned as an autonomous body, however, and the ideas expressed in its report are its own.

The memorandum which follows evolved from the discussions of the Committee over a period of three years, from ideas and text contributed by individual members, and from the voluminous and growing literature on learning and teaching. Throughout its deliberations, the Committee had at hand an extensive bibliography prepared under the direction of its Executive Director, Dr. James L. Jarrett. It was also aware of prior experimentation with college teaching, and of experiments in progress. The initial drafts of the memorandum were prepared by the Executive Director. The most advanced of these drafts was subsequently revised by the Chairman, in accordance with the Committee's suggestions. Much of the original version is incorporated in the published version, although sometimes in modified arrangement. The final editing was completed by Dr. Paul L. Ward, a member of the Committee.

The Committee on Undergraduate Teaching has been reasonably representative of the college and university community of the United States. It has had members from large universities with distinguished research records and from four-year liberal arts colleges, widely distributed geographically. Some of its members had had experience in the state colleges and universities. Unfortunately, it has had no direct representation from the junior colleges or community colleges, although several members of the committee had worked with representatives of these colleges. Most broad fields of learning and expression were represented, the arts being a regretted exception. Of such omissions the Committee was conscious. It sought by means of consultation to bring the ideas of all sectors of higher education to bear upon its consideration of the importance and improvement of teaching. In fact, the representatives of those disciplines and institutional types most thoroughly represented on the Committee would be the first to say that no discipline and no kind of college or university speaks with a single voice. In discussions of the Committee they certainly did not. There was a refreshing diversity of views.

The memorandum is addressed deliberately to the beginning undergraduate teachers. In the judgment of the Committee, it is they who need most to perceive the variety of opportunities and the freedom of choices that are available to them, as they begin the teaching which almost all of them feel strong concern to do well. It is they who may gain most from a discussion of the functions of college teaching, of institutional arrangements that affect these functions, and of strategies for achieving good teaching. They can be helped toward an understanding of their students, and can be helped to perceive their opportunities to learn from and work with their faculty and administrative colleagues. Theirs in particular is the opportunity to bring fresh ideas to teaching; and theirs is the power to determine the level and quality of teaching in the next generation.

The Committee recognizes, of course, that what may be of immediate concern to beginning undergraduate teachers will also hold interest for their more experienced colleagues, and for their deans and presidents. Only the academically inexperienced person, or the naive one, would believe that good teaching can prosper, no matter how able and earnest the beginning teacher, unless the conditions for its nurture are provided by the faculty as a whole, by the administrative officers, and by the governing boards. The concluding chapter of the memorandum is on this theme, and is addressed to all who can give sustenance and support to good teaching.

I cannot conclude this foreword without expressing my great appreciation for the time, thought, and judgment given over three years by the members of the Committee. I am grateful to the Executive Director for having brought that thought to focus by putting a memorandum to paper, and to all who helped assemble materials or facilitate the meetings of the Committee.

Finally, I must express the hope of the Committee that this memorandum will prove helpful in the colleges and universities, and that it will advance, in some measure, the cause of good teaching.

C. Easton Rothwell, *Chairman*

Introduction

The concern of this committee to emphasize the importance of teaching in the colleges and universities, and to help foster its improvement, grows from an awareness of great need and great opportunity. The need is acute because our society requires, as never before, a broad infusion of well-educated minds. It requires also, greater numbers of students sufficiently motivated to devote their careers to advancing the academic disciplines and the practical expression of these disciplines through teaching and the other professions.

The need is made more acute by the low priority given to teaching at present in too many colleges and universities as compared with other claims upon the professor's time. It is likewise made more acute by the burgeoning of college and university attendance, which, if we project present trends, will more than double before the end of the century.

The opportunity to improve teaching is at least as great as the need for it. An impatient expectation of good teaching has spread widely in the present student generation. At the same time, there is more practical recognition in the universities that excellent teaching is essential, not only because it is an intrinsic function of the institution, but also because it is essential to the advancement of knowledge and because there is a reciprocal advantage between good teaching and good research, pure and applied.

Other elements in today's climate are also more conducive to good teaching. On some campuses, from coast to coast, bureaus and centers have been founded that are dedicated to the improvement of teaching. Many professional organizations and learned societies have begun to pay more attention to the needs for improved teaching, to develop programs of training and evaluation, and to publicize promising innovations in teaching approach. Important experiments in the preparation of undergraduate teachers are being sponsored by a handful of foundations. More awards for exceptional teaching are being given, within single institutions and by professional associations. Several organizations, including the American Council on Education, have held conferences to examine the problems of improving teaching. Moreover, serious research on learning and teaching at the college level has recently begun to increase markedly. There is a rapidly growing bibliography of perceptive and helpful books and articles on the subject.

In two other respects an environment more favorable to good teaching is developing. The recognized need for excellent instruction has prompted some universities and more colleges to provide the facilities and the patterns of academic obligation favorable to teaching. In these institutions, the expectation of teaching proficiency is often heightened by the priority given it in the granting of promotions and tenure. At the same time, the campus emphasis upon teaching has been abetted by the attention focused upon learning through the news media. This, in turn, has aroused concern among trustees and regents, legislators, the parents of high school students confronting a choice of colleges and the general public. These important constituencies of the colleges and universities are not only showing a greater interest in teaching, but are responding to and asserting higher standards for judging it.

Despite these encouraging trends, the great task of improving undergraduate teaching remains to be done. The importance of teaching needs to be more firmly and widely accepted. Our hope, therefore, in publishing this memorandum is to stir more interest and promote more discussion about the need, the problems, the possibilities, and the immense rewards of effective teaching. We address ourselves to men and women whose disciplinary knowledge is extensive and whose scholarship is impeccable. We turn especially to you who are new college teachers, still young in the profession, and to those of you still in graduate school but nearing the day when you will go to your first job. Your generation can make a vast difference in college teaching during the next few years. Although you would be ill-advised to ignore the tensions that will continue to exist between teaching, on the one hand, and research, consultation, and other academic activities on the other, you can make a major contribution. You cannot only find for yourselves a satisfying, mutually helpful, and creative relationship between teaching and other activities, principally research; you can help make this evident to others. In doing so, you cannot only discover the great freedom of conception and application available to every teacher; you can give it new dimension. In doing so, you can help arouse the latent and widespread concern for the teaching arts.

We see teaching as a process continuous with scholarship, informed by it and in turn stimulating its pursuit. We view teaching as a source of deep satisfaction to those who have cultivated its practice and discovered their own distinctive styles. We know from experience that good teaching is not only compatible with the many other preoccupations of today's professors, but that, like scholarship, it both informs them and benefits from them. The comingling of activities increasingly characteristic of today's undergraduate teachers is proving to be a boon and a new way of life in our colleges and universities.

We agree with Erik Erikson when he speaks of a need to teach "not only for the sake of those who need to be taught, and not only for the sake of the teacher's identity, but because facts are kept alive by being told, logic by being demonstrated, truth by being professed." Erikson speaks of human beings as the "teaching species," so that not the professional teacher alone, but "every mature adult knows the satisfaction of explaining what is dear to him and of being understood by a groping mind."[1]

The plan of the following memorandum is a simple one. We first examine the present and prospective situations on the American campus as they affect learning and teaching, and draw attention to changes that are in progress or may take place in the future. We then consider the choices open to the young teacher today as to where, under what conditions, and how he may practice his profession. We explore ways in which he may conceive his teaching role, models he may follow, strategy and tactics he may employ, and procedures and relationships available to him. Central to these considerations is the relationship between the young professor, the student, and the subject matter, and this relationship we explore in some detail.

We then turn to two controversial but related topics, the preparation of teachers and the evaluation of teaching. Finally, we move to the larger conception of the college professor, recognizing that to understand him as a teacher, it is necessary to see him simultaneously as scholar and pursuer of research, consulting expert, public servant, and often, within his own institution, committeeman and politician. When he is concerned about good teaching, he can do much on its behalf by exerting his talents and his influence in an appropriate manner in the deliberations and the decisions of the faculty, the administration, and, where acceptable, the students.

We believe that the need for improved undergraduate teaching is an urgent and important one. We believe the present opportunities to bring it about are great. We enter the effort to realize those opportunities with ideas drawn from the experience of many teachers and institutions, including our own, and with many questions. As we explore these questions, some provisional answers emerge. We hope these questions and our tentative answers will provoke others to probe and respond further. At the conclusion of the memorandum, we present a list of the principal ideas it contains, ideas born of the questions and of our quest for answers.

1 The Teaching Environment: Present and Future

The young scholar emerging from graduate school too seldom asks himself or his prospective employer what is the teaching environment of the institution to which he thinks of going. We believe that he should not only ask this, among other questions, but that given the rapidity of educational change today, he should attempt to find out what may be the future conditions of teaching.

The environment of teaching must be construed broadly, of course. It ranges from the size, character, tradition, and climate of the institution to such specifics as salary and benefits, prospective advancement, teaching schedules and loads, library adequacy, and the availability of other teaching aids and facilities. It is affected by the nature and quality of students, faculty and administrators, and by such semi-specific things as the expectations of the institution about scholarship, teaching, and other functions. Nor does the range of environmental factors stop here. It must include forces exerted upon the college or university from the outside, or more positively the relations between the institution and the community, from the local to the national level, together with the attitudes of the institution toward the participation of the young teacher in this process. There are many more elements. Let us examine some on the list.

Diversity and growth

It is patently impossible to speak in one breath of all institutions of higher learning, because of their diversity. This every beginning college teacher and graduate student knows. The spectrum is broad, and the potential for teaching varies even within its narrower segments. A recent

13

Harvard study identifies four main types of institutions:

1. The research-oriented universities—perhaps twenty to forty of them.
2. The liberal arts colleges devoted to the development of "the whole man and scholar" who is going on to advanced education—probably fifty to seventy-five of them.
3. Colleges devoted to producing an educated citizenry—the investigators allege most colleges fall in this type.
4. Colleges and universities devoted to specialized instruction and the cultivation of specialized skills—one hundred twenty or so of them.

To these categories, all of which may be represented within a single composite like Columbia University, another rapidly growing category must be added:

5. Junior colleges and community colleges—which often assume a distinctive responsibility for adult education.

Among large universities, public and private, there are important differences, in offerings, in emphases, in quality. These are apparent, even in a perusal of catalogues. Within the trade they are known in even more subtle dimension. The same may be said of state colleges and technical schools. Among the institutions that are classed as liberal arts colleges or universities there are even more striking differences, as a study conducted by a member of this committee has made clear. The study focused upon twelve colleges from Berea to Amherst and disclosed twelve readily identifiable sub-types. Even within universities and colleges, the concern for teaching and the improvement of teaching varies from department to department. Obviously, therefore, it is difficult if not dangerous to generalize about teaching in higher education. It is equally difficult, without careful inquiry, to determine the kind of institution in which one wishes to teach, or to choose among institutions where positions may be open.

Since 1946 there has been a vast increase in the number of students who attend college, and a consequent burgeoning in the size and number of colleges and universities. This trend, which has caused the college population almost to double in less than a decade, shows no sign of abating. There will be some fluctuations, but undergraduate enrollments, approximately six million in 1967-68, will probably grow to about fifteen million by the year 2000. One astute observer points out that "if all existing institutions doubled in size during the last third of the century, even then we would still need about 1,000 new four-year institutions and perhaps as many as 2,000 new junior colleges to handle the projected expansion."[2]

The growth will not be even, of course. In some regions it will very much exceed others. The publicly supported colleges and universities will grow more rapidly in number and size than the privately supported ones. In today's spectrum, institutions range in size from small private colleges of one hundred students to vast universities of forty thousand. In the third of a century ahead the present preponderance of small and middle-sized institutions among the more than two thousand that now exist will be challenged as the overall average size rises perceptibly.

What does this trend mean for teaching? First, of course, it means that there will be jobs. Even though the production of doctorates is also increasing, the needs of the colleges and universities, despite the growing drain of Ph.D.'s to business, government and other professions, will sustain a lively demand for teachers. Until at least the mid-1970's, there will continue to be a seller's market. This, in turn, will mean sustained or higher salaries and corollary benefits. It will help to bring about a reduction of teaching loads, much needed in some colleges and universities. It may lead to improved sabbatical policies. Almost certainly it will have the effect of enhancing the status of the young college teacher.

The broad choice of institutions now confronting the young scholar will grow broader. Among the essentially liberal arts institutions, whether they be colleges or small universities, there will be an even greater range of sizes and types. There will be many more universities or state colleges of from fifteen to twenty-five thousand students. There will be more and more institutions designed to achieve smallness and intimacy in the interests of learning, either in the midst of bigness, as at Santa Cruz and at Monteith of Wayne State, or as off-shoots of bigness, as at the Oakland campus of Michigan State University. There will also be a very rapid growth of junior colleges, as evidenced by the founding of one hundred and fourteen such colleges during a recent five-year period when eight new universities and forty-four new state colleges and liberal arts colleges were established. Moreover, there will be a trend, already evident, toward achieving more stature and autonomy for the junior college and toward the upgrading of its faculty.

Growth is producing changes within established institutions. The abundance of entering students has led to greater selectivity, even among public institutions which only a few years ago boasted that they never turned away the sons and daughters of state taxpayers. Some public institutions admit only the top eighth of the high school graduates; private institutions are even more selective. The levels of intellectual concern in these institutions have risen accordingly. Various ways are being found, however, to open the doors of higher education to any aspiring young man or woman. In California this is achieved through a hierarchy among institutions. Any high school graduate may enter a junior college, and, if capable, ultimately transfer to a four-year institution. About one third of the students may enter the state colleges and one eighth the university.

Pressures on education

Forces other than growth are producing changes in the teaching situation. New intellectual and social needs, growing from the large and rapid expansion of knowledge, the discovery of new theories and methods for organizing and interpreting knowledge, the demand for greater opportunities for minority groups, and the ever-closer relationships between the campus and society, whether local, national, or international have all made their impact felt in institutions of every kind and size. As a result, there have been changes in curriculum, in conceptions of how education, and particularly liberal education, can best be achieved in the undergraduate years, and in teaching approaches. For educational reasons, as well as for reasons of economy, as costs of learning rise, the college calendar is changing. As a result of these changes, and others external to the educational program, opportunities for choice in discharging educational responsibilities are changing and growing. There are also important changes in the whole pattern of college and university governance.

Relationships of the undergraduate college with the secondary schools and the graduate schools on either side of it are also changing. At the lower level, the quality and depth of instruction have so improved in some secondary schools that the colleges and universities are able to eliminate some freshman year work for graduates of those schools. This trend is growing. The influence of the graduate schools on the undergraduate curriculum is more than keeping step with the proportion of graduates, now over 50%, who continue their studies beyond four years. Out of what is perhaps too frequently a correct appraisal of graduate school requirements, some undergraduate faculties have moved toward greater specialization in the junior and senior years. One hears with increasing frequency the assertion that liberal education should be obtained in the freshman and sophomore years, perhaps in combination with the senior year of high school, leaving the upperclass years freer for specialization. This is said despite the actual preference of some graduate departments for students with broad undergraduate training.

Larger numbers of undergraduates aiming at graduate education tend, in any event, to concentrate in their major fields and to work for grades acceptable to graduate schools. Needless to say, these trends attenuate the content and spirit of liberal learning as it has been conceived and organized until now. They are not, however, sufficient evidence to support the dire prediction that the undergraduate liberal arts college will disappear.

The job of the professor is changing also. He is apt not only to be a rigorously trained scholar, but also to be more knowledgeable about foundations and government agencies than was his predecessor of just a few years ago. In the universities more than in most colleges he may be less acquainted with his campus colleagues beyond his own department than with his disciplinary colleagues on far away campuses. Again, in the universities more than in the colleges, he may spend as much time away from the campus as he does in teaching. Much of his committee work will be done away from the institution rather than on the campus. As an Amherst report has pointed out, no longer is it true that even "where the faculty lives within easy reach of the campus, close attachments are fostered, students are encouraged to drop in at their teachers' homes for tea or dinner, and faculty members often spend convivial evenings in fraternity houses."[3] The trend is otherwise. As one member of this committee has written: "The strong college of the future will not frown on, but cherish, faculty who consult for the government, take research leaves, and run up monstrous longdistance phone bills."[4] As subsequent sections of this memorandum seek to make plain, this kind of multiple activity is not necessarily incompatible with good teaching, but in fact can enhance it. And incidentally, the multiple activities of today's professor often place him in a better position to obtain improvements in salary and emoluments, rank, instructional load, teaching assignments, student and clerical assistance, and library and laboratory resources.

In several different ways, the college and university are getting a different kind of student today than a decade ago. A significant number of students are coming in with less background. Yet in almost all institutions, the majority are more capable. They show evidence of the improved elementary and secondary education they have received. Almost everywhere they have greater intellectual and social concerns and deeper commitment. Among large numbers of them, as young teachers know, there is an urge to convert learning into action. This mood not only challenges existing curricular concepts and teaching approaches, but has also made an impact upon the governance of colleges and universities. It likewise influences, sometimes profoundly and often creatively, the relationship between the campus and the community. Without question, today's students are a more interesting and stimulating group to teach than were many of their predecessors.

The present emphasis upon social equality is felt in the colleges and universities also. The response to it takes different forms. In one state there has been a move to distribute financial assistance in public institutions in a manner that would enable any child, from whatever economic status, to attend college or university provided he can qualify. This move has been tempered by the decision to insist upon excellence as well as opportunity. In select private colleges there have been deliberate experiments with new methods of student recruitment. Evidence that the standard admission criteria—grade point averages and test scores—are importantly influenced by environment, has prompted several colleges and universities to seek talented young men and women by other means. The quest has succeeded and the results of educating these students have been, on the whole, gratifying.

Changing procedures

Two of the fences that have delimited the college and the university are coming down. One pertains to space, the other to time. Increasingly, the single college or university is ceasing to provide the sole site for the undergraduate education of a single student. Rather it provides a home base, and in some ways serves as a switching station. Part of the education may be on overseas campuses, in community internships, in work opportunities, or in special programs at other institutions, either during the academic year or in the summer. Through a deliberate pooling of resources in some associations of colleges, and by a growing number of arrangements between individual institutions, some undergraduates are working simultaneously or sequentially in two places to achieve programs that could not be wholly achieved in either. Education is likewise being enriched by bringing additional resources to the institution through inter-library arrangements, by telelecture and television, by the increasing use of guest lecturers and visiting professors, by the return of faculty deliberately encouraged to travel and study away from the campus, and by other means.

On their part, the students are stretching or contracting the normal four years of undergraduate education as their interests and circumstances require, sometimes for travel and special work elsewhere, some-times simply to gain a breathing spell—and some dollars—on a job.

None of these trends is wholly new. In fact, there is a centuries-old tradition of both student and faculty itinerancy. What is happening currently is simply more diverse and more deliberately planned, and is facilitated by the increased mobility in contemporary society and by technological improvements such as the airplane, the long-distance tele-phone call, computers and computer extensions, and television.

Other mechanical devices and human arrangements have also pro-vided inventive means of easing the drudgery connected with teaching, or of increasing its effectiveness. The tape recorder for the professor's evaluation of student papers, increased use of student self-testing, and the bringing in of teaching interns, both for the intelligent relief of the professor and for the intelligent training of the intern, are examples of how this is being accomplished.

Interest in teaching

One more factor of considerable importance to the beginning college teacher is the change in the climate toward teaching, both within the academic community and outside it. The undeniably increasing concern of the students themselves for good teaching, manifested through their own evaluations, some good, some bad, of faculty performance through their statements, and through their demonstrations shows no evidence of diminishing, and will probably be a continuing force. There is encour-agement in the increased concern of the universities to assist in pre-paring good teachers. Harvard, Yale, Columbia, Michigan, Virginia, California are in the list of institutions which have recorded their con-cern for teaching and have done something about improving and recognizing it. Max Wise reports that more than fifteen universities have asked the Danforth Foundation whether it could provide financial assist-ance calculated to transform the usual teaching assistantship into a more substantial internship. He acknowledges that the interest of graduate faculty members is not uniform, but says that a substantial and influ-ential part of the graduate faculties of these universities have a new recognition of their responsibilities for improved teaching.[5]

Contrary to the repeated allegation that the graduate schools not only fail to train teachers, but even destroy the motivation for undergraduate teaching, evidence gathered by the Danforth Foundation shows little negative effect. At the same time it shows insufficient positive effort by the graduate schools to improve teaching, and even a denial by some members of the graduate faculties that their schools or departments have any responsibility to prepare their incipient Ph.D.'s for teaching. Except in a few institutions, the beginning professor emerges from graduate work deficient in almost all the skills of teaching: the formulation of goals, curriculum and course construction, an understanding of student differences, the development of a good lecture, the conduct of lively discussion, the adequate use of teaching aids, the evaluation of students. Even so, the evidence shows an increase in the emphasis on teaching, and it is reasonable to say that without the improvements in knowledge and in the canons of objective scholarship fostered at the graduate level, undergraduate teaching would be much the poorer.

The colleges also have a responsibility for the improvement of teaching. Though they pride themselves on their teaching function, too few colleges offer any real assistance to the beginning teacher other than the occasional counsel of a dean. In very many of them, the classroom experience is regarded as strictly private, and the young professor is put entirely on his own, when suggestions from an experienced and able teacher could be helpful and would in many cases be welcomed. It is refreshing to discover several colleges and universities that place their resources behind the effort to assist not only the preparation, but also the improvement of the young teacher. When this happens, it is normally the result not only of faculty determination, but also of leadership by presidents and deans, and of administrative facilitation.

The growing public interest in good teaching finds practical expression in the concern of trustees and regents and their willingness to support the presidents and faculties in experimentation. It finds expression in the shifting emphases of foundations. And it finds expression in government appropriations. In the deliberate effort to improve the teaching as well as the research in their institutions, the legislators of many states continue to vote ever-increasing appropriations. In some larger states, the tax bill for education at all levels is the greatest single item in the budget. There is no sign that this will cease to be the case.

An even more dramatic increase in spending on education is in prospect at the federal level. Whereas today all Washington agencies expend on all kinds and levels of education in excess of nine billion dollars, the prospect is that by 1975 that amount will at least have doubled and may be much greater, depending on other circumstances. There is every indication that substantial sums will be funneled specifically into the improvement of teaching.

This effort to sketch the present and future environment of undergraduate teaching has by no means been comprehensive. Rather it is suggestive. It cannot be concluded without comment on the attitudes of faculties toward the improvement of teaching. Generalizations here are especially dangerous. It can be said, however, that in most institutions those who will accept reasonable change and work for it are less numerous than those who are neutral or opposed. It is also safe to say that with many undeniable exceptions, the movement toward improved teaching in its many facets comes principally from the younger faculty, especially those emerging into positions of influence. Recognizing the tensions and resistances in faculty relations, they are still convinced that the system is open enough for individual initiatives.

We live in a period, however, when the context of every institution, large or small, is bound to be influenced by great forces at work in our society, and by the attitudes they are generating. The Peace Corps, Head Start, Vista, and comparable programs are sending many "alumni" to the colleges and universities with strong convictions about the importance of teaching, and of the human-to-human relationship so essential to it. The new egalitarianism that has emerged from both the civil rights and poverty programs is also lending momentum to the upsurge of reform tendencies within colleges and universities, and particularly among young faculty. The earnest quest for relevance will produce efforts to bring scholarship and human meaning closer together. The millennium is certainly not at hand, either now or in the foreseeable future, but these trends and others akin to them will certainly lend impetus to the improvement of teaching throughout the whole spectrum of colleges and universities.

II The Opportunities and Roles of the Undergraduate Teacher

The beginning college teacher, with few exceptions, desires not only to teach but to teach well. He wishes also to continue his scholarship so as to advance within his discipline and his profession. Hence, he is aware that he must find an accommodation of both these interests and his way of academic life in whatever kind of college or university position he accepts. Some young teachers discover early that the accommodation can be a very creative one.

His choice of institution

As we explore the opportunities that confront the beginning undergraduate teacher, therefore, let us concentrate upon those at the heart of his professional concern: teaching, scholarship, and their fruitful interaction. These opportunities will obviously differ from institution to institution, according to kind, size, tradition, and current values and purposes. Fortunately for today's beginning college and university teacher, the choice of institutions before him is a reasonably broad one. One thoughtful investigator, who concludes that until the mid-1970's the demand for young teachers will exceed the supply and that thereafter jobs may be harder to find, puts it this way: "If one is a young college teacher, this is obviously a good time to be alive; and the late 1970's will be a good time to have achieved tenure."[6]

In choosing among institutions where positions may be available, the astute beginning teacher will look beyond nomenclature, beyond category, and make a hard assessment of the potential teaching situation and the opportunities for scholarly growth, as they bear on his particular case. He should seek out specific evidence. Reading of several

22

issues of the campus newspaper, or even better a few impromptu conversations at the campus coffee shop, can tell him something about the student clientele and the human situation with which he will be dealing. His own background may qualify him to do well and gain special satisfactions at the small denominational college, or with the first generation college students at the new state university. But he may want to weigh the practical chances that a position off the main line for careers can prove, by its fitness for him, a way of leapfrogging ahead if things go well—as has indeed been the case in a number of distinguished academic careers.

We hope, in addition, that he will examine the manner in which the college, university, or technical institute is responding to the great forces now affecting higher education. Making human allowances for negativist comments, he may still be able to judge from the remarks of his prospective colleagues whether the institution through its public-spirited efforts is tending to gain in vitality and generosity of spirit, and so to improve as a working environment.

The discriminating job-seeker will not be misled by appearances nor awed by reputation. David Riesman and Alan Cartter both have pointed out that appearances and reputation outlast reality, especially at the college level.[7] Intrinsic changes, whether for good or for bad, will not be reflected in the kinds of students and faculty attracted to the institution until some time after the changes have occurred. This social lag can have ill effects on all concerned. The consequences for the less prestigious college that is actually lifting its quality and performance under imaginative leadership should not be discouraging, as it waits for reputation to catch up with what it is doing. Among the universities, overall status, very much influenced by graduate teaching and research, too often outweighs both the opportunities for undergraduate teaching and its quality as the magnet attracting both students and faculty. Of this the astute young Ph.D. will be aware. He will recognize that if he is fortunate enough to obtain a teaching position at a college or university with high reputation, he is still confronted with the same dilemma: how to teach undergraduates well, how to get on with his scholarship, how to reconcile these most effectively, and how to get recognition for doing all three things.

As we consider in more detail how this dilemma may be resolved in different kinds of institutions, it is necessary to remember that no generalization can be adequate for about 2,200 institutions of varying size, organization, function, and quality during a period of great educational growth and change. As we speak of small colleges, for example, we must not forget that some large universities are experimenting with ways to achieve the values of smallness whether through a cluster college plan, by means of the liberal college outpost, in "living-learning" residence halls, or through other device. We must bear in mind that many publicly-supported state colleges, and some private liberal arts colleges which have always stressed teaching, are putting increasing emphasis on faculty research. And we must not forget that in both large and small institutions, the teaching and learning process (as well as that of research) is being importantly affected by developments in technology.

To the beginning college teacher, several factors that will affect the teaching situation are of immediate importance. At the center of them is the concern of the institution about good undergraduate teaching, and the manner in which it recognizes quality in the classroom. Beyond this central consideration, the young teacher is, or ought to be, asking about teaching loads, class schedules, course opportunities, feasible teaching approaches, library adequacy, the facilities and equipment available for course or laboratory, and similar matters. Let us consider some of them.

In general, the smaller colleges will place greater value on teaching, especially undergraduate teaching, than will the larger institutions. They consider their primary role to be that of inducing learning, and they regard smallness and a close relationship between student and teacher as essential to that end. Except by stressing their low student-teacher ratio and small classes, however, too many colleges fail to make explicit either their conceptions of good teaching or their interest in ways to attain it and to reward it. Too often there is no orientation or preparation for the beginning teacher. He is left to learn by osmosis, or to struggle on with ineffective teaching approaches, hardening his attachment to them in the process. By contrast there are a few colleges, some prestigious, others not, that concern themselves actively with all aspects of teaching: the conception and planning of both curricula and courses, the intelligent use of teaching technology, the improvement of lecture, discussion, and seminar techniques, and the counseling and appraising of students. Some few afford in-service training in these and other matters. A very few, such as Antioch, ask members of their faculties to work with young teaching interns destined for other institutions.

Comparisons with larger institutions must be made carefully, lest they be misleading. The fact that a large public university has a 26/1 student-teacher ratio by comparison with an 11/1 ratio in a neighboring liberal arts college or a 16/1 ratio at a nearby state college does not mean *ipso facto* that its concern with good teaching is less. It merely raises the question, to which the alert young teacher will seek an answer. In the particular university here referred to, he would discover strong evidences of concern for good undergraduate teaching both among the faculty and within the administration. He would discover also, and this may be no surprise, that although he may have to yield something in teaching intimacy in the university, he will have to teach fewer hours than he would in the college. Whereas university loads average six to eight contract hours weekly, those of most liberal arts colleges average nine to twelve, those of state colleges tend to be formally twelve though sometimes less, and those of junior colleges are still more numerous. In calculating teaching load, however, the inquiring young teacher will also quickly discover that although he has more contract hours weekly in the smaller college than he would have in the university, he also has fewer students. At the same moment, he may discover that the teaching intimacy on which the college prides itself will require more hours of consultation with students, thus offsetting the smaller numbers. All this he weighs against the amount of time that will remain to him for reading and research.

These two concerns, teaching and research, often become opposing demands and hard to reconcile. It would distort the facts to assert that at many major universities a concern with undergraduate teaching has the upper hand over the preoccupation with graduate work and research. Those who wish more attention to undergraduate teaching are often discouraged, so great are the urgencies on the other side. But it would likewise be a mistake to ignore the fact that an increasing number of university departments and colleges are experimenting in one form or another with improved approaches to undergraduate teaching. As indicated earlier, a substantial number of universities are seeking to improve the training of graduate students by intern programs, and these should help narrow the gap between graduate school and undergraduate teaching.

Conditions of teaching

Before turning to a discussion of the research and publication demands on young teachers, let us consider two other matters that will have considerable effect upon their happiness or unhappiness in teaching: the kinds of programs and schedules they may have, and the nature of their faculty associates, in the larger institutions and in the smaller. We shall leave until later in the memorandum a consideration of library resources, physical facilities, and equipment.

It is difficult to generalize about the courses a young member of the faculty may be able to teach or may have to teach. Especially in large departments of large institutions, the beginner may have to take one or more sections of the survey course shunned by his more senior colleagues, or at least participate in the staff handling of the subject. If he is fortunate, he may be able to offer a small class or seminar in his own field. But in his first years he may have to teach courses listed in the catalogue that lie some distance from the focus of his own interests. These may conceivably turn out to be for him valuable introductions to worthwhile subjects, or to have been precisely the fresh experience he needed to get on his feet as a teacher. But a course load he would not have chosen is less easy to turn to good account if he is confronted at the same time with such discouragements as serious intra-departmental tensions and infighting, or a smug department's resistance to any innovation whatever, or a domineering and restrictive department head.

In various ways, that is, he must accept the beginner's lot. Such circumstances should not long discourage the beginning teacher, however. There is almost never anything to prevent him from putting new wine into the old bottles of existing courses. Nor is the young professor assigned to a "bread and butter" departmental course prevented from arguing his preferences concerning content, organization, readings, or laboratory requirements. Even in multisectioned courses he may find room for the expression of his own intellectual approaches. For example, in the Humanities and the Contemporary Civilization courses at Columbia College, although all sections are studying Montaigne, the professor from the French Department may be exploring literary influence, whereas the professor from the Philosophy Department will be conducting a close analysis of Montaigne's thought, and the professor of History is concerned with the author as an embodiment of Renaissance individualism. Many other institutions have similar courses, and the opportunity they offer for individualizing teaching is an opportunity to be seized.

We have been describing conditions that may confront the young teacher in a large university. Interestingly enough, the same kinds of constraints exist in small colleges, though in slightly different form. In the presence of smaller departments and too frequently an over-long list of catalogue offerings, the newest assistant professor must frequently carry courses that he would not select if given free choice. Nevertheless, the level of flexibility in the small college is such that course content can readily be modified, and virtually every member of the faculty should have opportunity to teach within the sphere of his own interests. Under a more recent trend, manifest in both the college and the university, professors, young as well as old, are deliberately being offered opportunity to present at least one course or seminar in their own fields. This is under the assumption that the rigidly-structured curriculum may be a mistake, and that more learning, together with more intellectual excitement, will result when teachers lead students into subjects at the heart of the teacher's interest.

We shall have more to say about course content and teaching approaches, but let us pause to recognize intellectual and disciplinary companionship as an essential stimulus to teaching. Most young teachers hunger for association with colleagues in their own disciplines. Discourses with them is obviously a means of checking one's own judgments, sharpening one's perceptions, gaining stimulation. This hunger will be better satisfied normally in the large institution than in the small, whether it be university, college, or technical institute. Not infrequently, the beginning college teacher may also expect and find greater satisfaction where graduate work is combined with undergraduate. On the other hand, the very size of the larger institution militates against much cross-departmental or cross-disciplinary communication among colleagues, whereas this tends to be unavoidable, and often fruitful, in smaller colleges. When the university professor looks beyond his department (which may be at least half as large as the total full-time faculty of a college) he inclines to turn for further stimulation to his professional association. The professor in the small college, by contrast, cannot escape an awareness of the whole faculty and the range of its intellectual concerns, unless he happens to be a recluse. For this reason, cross-disciplinary ventures tend to come about more naturally in the college. And by the same token, the college faculty has more occasion to be on the alert against superficiality.

Adjustment of goals

Despite the intrinsic concern to teach and teach well that the young assistant professor brings to his first position, he must quickly find his own modus vivendi for the reconciling of teaching and scholarly growth. It is our hope that as he finds that solution, he will accord teaching the priority it deserves as an essential ingredient of scholarly growth and of advancement within his discipline. This is not to say that the young teacher will not and should not seek to establish his professional identity by creative work in this discipline, whether through research, painting or composing, or other means. There will be distinct advantage to his teaching, fully as much as to his academic status, when he is able to say with the pride of one whose work has gained notice, "I am a botanist," "I am a linguist" or "I am a composer."

To be sure, promotion and tenure decisions are made in considerable measure on the basis of "productivity" and "visibility" at many major universities. Even in some state colleges and in an increasing number of liberal arts colleges, evidence of creative work in one's discipline is in ever greater measure one criterion for advancement. In a period of acute competition for able faculty, this trend is to be expected. Some years ago Logan Wilson was able to state that "except in perhaps forty or fifty major universities at the outside, the 'publish or perish' dictum . . . is largely a myth. If it were widely in force, most faculty persons would be out of jobs."[8] Although this situation is changing, it continues to be true that fewer than 10% of the nationwide faculty account for more than 90% of published research.

It is a fact, nonetheless, that in institutions where graduate work is important, publication or its equivalent is an aid to advancement, and that the expectation of production is spreading to the four-year colleges. Even if this kind of incentive were reduced, however, the genuinely able young scholar would almost certainly wish to sustain his research and his creative effort because of his own intellectual curiosity and his own inner drives. If he is worth his salt, he values the recognition that fine, original work brings him within his discipline, and even more widely in both the academic and the lay worlds.

There has been much recent criticism of the graduate schools for emphasis on research and publication at the expense of teaching. Some of this criticism is justified. Even as we press for good undergraduate teaching and its appropriate recognition, however, we acknowledge the stature which graduate institutions have given to objective scholarship and pure creativity. We do so because of our conviction that teaching in the highest sense at whatever level in our system of education must have behind it the spirit of creative adventure, of search and discovery. It must have also the skills with which to serve imaginative and solid intellectual adventure. On the other hand, we hold to the conviction that any failure to relate research to teaching, or any pursuit of it at the deliberate neglect of good teaching, can be a disservice to one's discipline, and especially to students who will carry forward that discipline in the generation ahead. It is, in broadest terms, a disservice to the educational well-being of our society. As we consider teaching approaches and models, we can draw upon the experience of distinguished scholars who have also been great teachers to illustrate what the wedding of the finest research spirit with the greatest teaching inclination can mean.

Meanwhile we suggest there is at times positive advantage for the professor deeply involved in research in having to extend his teaching beyond the immediate concerns of his inquiry. Wilburt McKeachie has put it, "not only teaching but research itself suffers when a professor is no longer required to keep up with, and integrate, new developments in areas related to but not directly involved in his own research."[9] He cites a study of scientists with the doctorate in universities and governmental laboratories of whom it was found that those spending more than three-fourths time on research were less productive as scientists than those spending less time on research and more time teaching or in administration.[10] This was true both for junior and senior scientists.

Decisions about teaching

We have tried to make clear that the beginning undergraduate teacher cannot always choose his courses, nor even teach them, in a manner that will enable him to inter-link most fruitfully his research and his teaching. As he progresses in seniority, the linkage may be easier to achieve. From the very beginning, however, he can so teach that his deepest intellectual concerns will strike fire in the flowering concerns of his students. Let us examine some of the teaching approaches available to the young professor, some of the models he may use as guides for his performance.

Teaching is a process much broader than the techniques employed in lecture hall, classroom, laboratory, or studio. It is broader than the preparation a teacher must make, or than any specific tasks required of the student. At its best, teaching entails the planning of a whole educational program, and of a specific course or other learning activity in that program. It involves the skillful evaluation of learning, not for the purpose of grading alone, but principally for assisting the student. At the foundation of all teaching, good or bad, lies some concept of what must be learned, of how best learning takes place, of the role both the teacher and the student have in this process. Let us begin by considering the foundation concepts and work our way toward the equally important subject of the specific techniques and skills required for the carrying out of these concepts.

There is a widely practiced tendency to regard undergraduate education as merely the transmission of culture. This conventional concept at its worst implies passivity on the part of the student and a "laying out of the subject" by the professor. In whatever setting, lecture or discussion or laboratory, the student can become a mere receptor for facts and interpretations set forth at the morning class by the authors of the books he reads, in the manual he uses. Beginning teachers seldom approach the task in this negative manner because of their own high motivation. When they do, it may be because of such preoccupation with their own efforts that they fail to perceive that learning is an active process in which both the student and the teacher must play roles, the teacher hopefully a diminishing one. Far from merely transmitting culture, the task of faculty is to invoke what Gordon Allport has termed the distinctive goal of higher education, "to inspect and criticize, to improve and increase this cultural cumulation." Beyond piquing the students' interest and filling their heads, therefore, the perceptive young professor will wish at the same time to help them improve their learning capacities and skills. He will try to help them carry on their own investigations, generate plausible hypotheses, verify, disprove or modify these in a scientific manner, reach warranted conclusions. He will help them improve their capacities for intelligent criticism, extend their perspectives, deepen their perceptions, heighten their sensitivities, release their creative impulses.

In describing the special task of the undergraduate college, Daniel Bell has said provocatively:

> As between the secondary school, with its emphasis upon primary skills and factual data, and the graduate or professional school, whose necessary concern is with specialization and technique, the distinctive function of the college is to deal with the grounds of knowledge. . . . The college can be the unique place where students acquire self-consciousness, historical consciousness, methodological consciousness.[11]

Good undergraduate education, therefore, means much more than any passive transmission of culture. It means the active involvement of students, on and off campus, in the process of learning. It means the stirring of motivation, one of the most crucial elements in learning. It means sufficient attention to the student to assist him in cultivating his individual style of learning, precisely as the young professor himself is cultivating his own style of teaching. Morris Keeton has summed it up in this manner:

> If we gave up "covering material" as our objective, in the interest of maximum motivation; if we provided as convenient as possible access to knowledge *when needed by the students*; if we permitted the role of individuality and individual style in learning and teach-

ing to be what it needs to be; if we respected the different modes of intellection . . . ; and if we provided a really active interplay between direct experience of the world and reflection upon that world —we would have a revolution in the way we teach.[12]

When the learning process is regarded passively, and even sometimes when it is not, the program of undergraduate education tends to be viewed as an aggregation or succession of courses. There is then a tendency among faculty to place much greater emphasis upon the subject taught than upon the learning desired. If the objective is a student possessed of usable knowledge and understanding in reasonable depth, of disciplined intellect and cultivated taste, of the capacity for creative expression, and of sufficient initiative to keep on growing, curricula and courses can be built, and indeed have been built to attain that object. The roles of the teacher then begin to emerge more clearly as facilitating ones. This implies no derogation of the young professor's scholarly capacities or aspirations. On the contrary, it can enhance them, as we shall attempt to show.

Let us view the young college teacher in four of the roles he inevitably plays: student of his students, exemplar of the educated man, expert in his discipline and special area of study, and master of teaching approaches calculated to achieve the "object desired," as we have just defined it.

Studying one's students

The wise young teacher of undergraduates will quickly recognize that he must give some time and attention to the study of his students. In the carrying out of his primary purpose, which is to bring about among them an intelligent understanding of the course he teaches and of his discipline, he will very soon be confronted with one of the elementary laws of learning, that the building of new comprehension must always start with what the student brings to the teaching situation. In conference with students, or through their papers, he will discover how far he may have misapprehended their backgrounds. He may at first be disillusioned when he learns that what he had regarded as an illuminating metaphor was taken literally by a good portion of the class, or that an illustration was remembered by nearly everyone in neglect of the principle it was intended to clarify. Or he may discover, as did one young professor, that his students were bored with his lectures and discussions because he was repeating materials to which they had already been exposed in secondary school, a circumstance that will be increas-

ingly common as our high schools continue to improve. If he is sufficiently sensitive to the human beings with whom he is working, he will
soon learn that it is a far greater sin to talk down to them than to talk
over their heads. And gradually, as he watches their faces and listens
to their impulsive comments, he will begin to find the level at which he
must approach them, and the range on either side of that level necessary
to accommodate the spread of capacities and backgrounds in his class.
In some situations it is possible to discover these things by tests properly
constructed. As a result of diagnostic tests, for example, many chemistry
departments have found it not only possible but necessary to elevate the
levels of freshman instruction.

Not infrequently the beginning college teacher rightly considers himself at an advantage over his older colleagues in being closer to the age
of his students. This may produce some shock as he discovers that
during his immersion in graduate studies he has lost touch with the
freshman or sophomore in late adolescence. He may actually have to
begin afresh to learn who and what his students are, what brings them
to college and keeps them there. He must discover what their problems
are and which of the great problems of society are meaningful to them.

Fortunately we are gaining greater insight into the college undergraduate through numerous studies of his being and his behavior. In
one study, Nevitt Sanford has characterized college freshmen as being
typically "authoritarian personalities," at least in a mild sense. Though
they may seem relatively stable and happy, they are apt to be stereo-
typed in their thinking, intolerant of ambiguity, submissive toward the
powerful and dominant toward the weak, unsure of their own abilities,
given to depression when faced with reverses, and well organized and
well behaved. Such students tend to change considerably by the time
they are seniors, losing much of their compulsiveness, and becoming
both more tolerant and more rebellious, more liberal, more unconven-
tional, but also perhaps less stable and happy. The freshman stands in
need of adult models, particularly young adults who show themselves to
him not simply as classroom teachers but also as human beings.[13]

The study of students is not restricted, however, to finding out what
is the level of their maturity or the depth of their knowledge and perception. As the young man or woman moves from high school to the
new styles and techniques of learning expected at the college level
(granted that the range of difference is steadily narrowing), he or she
can be greatly helped by the discerning professor. Many students remember with gratitude those professors who taught them something
important about how, and how not, to write a paper, or frame a blue-

book answer, or separate the parts of a complex question. Many also appreciate suggestions about such fundamental things as the taking of notes, the intelligent use of reference tools in the library, methods of going about research. Almost invariably the student will be grateful for special help in understanding a perplexing concept, a baffling problem. The study of the student, a rewarding process in terms of teaching result, never ceases to be necessary. It is practiced by professors who with frequency find themselves on the lists of men and women singled out by college students for their teaching competence.

Serving as exemplar

Let us look next at the teacher as exemplar. In this role, the teacher is saying, frequently without being conscious of it, "Watch how I work and do likewise in your own way." This is common enough in mathematics, where the professor often works through a proof, not just to show the outcome but to reveal the procedure, the way he makes derivations, and to exemplify elegance rather than cumbersomeness in the style of the proof. The teacher of painting may sit at his student's canvas and paint a while, not just to help him over a rough spot, but to show how an experienced artist goes about tackling such a problem. The scientist continually shows how he uses laboratory equipment to conduct an experiment, to refine an observation. The teacher of literature may analyze a poem or read one of his own, the philosopher may work through the central concepts in a paragraph, or the anthropologist may describe how he went about gaining essential information about a village, all as means of bringing to the student examples of the professional at work.

One eminent historian talking about another, Carl Lotus Becker on his teacher, Frederick Jackson Turner, reveals clearly this sense of exemplification:

> From the moment Turner ceased to figure in my mind as a teacher, I began to learn something from him. Not "teacher" but "historian" he was, better still "author", whose main occupation it was, not to teach us, but to be deeply engaged in research preliminary to the writing of notable books.

*   *   *   *   *   *

> An ordered body of information I could get, and did afterwards get, for myself; but from no other man did I ever get in quite the same measure that sense of watching a first-class mind at work on its own account, and not merely rehearsing for the benefit of others; the most delightful sense in the world of sitting there waiting for ideas to be

born; expectantly waiting for secret meanings, convenient explanatory hypotheses to be discovered, lurking as like as not under the dullest mass of drab facts ever seen.[14]

Another observer lauds the well-conceived and well-delivered lecture on the grounds that the student learns not necessarily or solely because a certain body of material is taught, but more because of the valuable human intellectual effort being made and observed. He cites James Russell Lowell's reaction to an Emerson lecture at Harvard: "We do not go to hear what Emerson says so much as to hear Emerson."[15] As in the case of David Starr Jordan whose introductory course on "Evolution" was always taken by great numbers of Stanford students in order to obtain a "course on Jordan," the man, the mind and the scholar at work are both model and inspiration.

Specifically, the great teacher at his best moments exemplifies much more than his knowledge and his methods of work. He shows not only how he attacks a problem, what tools he uses and how he uses them, but also where he looks for help from those who have gone before him. He displays also, perhaps unconsciously, the special concerns of his discipline, as revealed in what he looks for and what he can, for his purposes, ignore. He manifests an attitude of profound inquiry, perhaps surprising his students by taking seriously some things that they had regarded as trivial. By the standards he displays toward evidence and his rigorously disciplined handling of data, he may help his students to sense and share the contempt in which the scholar holds any dishonesty in research. He may also infect his students with his own delight in even small discoveries, in the beauty of a comprehensive explanation, in the freshness of an ingenious hypothesis.

Not all fields lend themselves equally well to exemplification in its several forms. Yet no field by its very nature forbids teaching by exemplification. And there can be no doubt that the exemplar carries much more conviction when he is being most true to the dictates of his own inquiring or creative mind, and to the most fundamental demands of his discipline. William Arrowsmith puts the need for exemplary teaching in vivid language:

> It is *men* we need now, not programs. . . . The humanities stand or fall according to the human worth of the man who professes them. . . . Charisma in a teacher is not a mystery or nimbus of personality, but radiant exemplification to which the student contributes a correspondingly radiant hunger for becoming.[16]

What Professor Arrowsmith says about humanists can readily be adapted to every major field of learning and endeavor. What he implies is essential for effective exemplification, is to surmount any inclination to contrive to be exemplary, and instead to carry out one's intellectual or creative task so effectively that its performance is inherently a compelling example. Whitehead gave the same intrinsic meaning to the exemplary function of the teacher, though in slightly different concept: "It should be the chief aim of a university professor to exhibit himself in his own true character—that is, as an ignorant man thinking, actively utilizing his small share of knowledge."[17]

Being the expert

We shall have more to say about the example of "man thinking" as we examine now in greater depth the relation between teaching and research. This leads us to the role of the teacher as expert in his discipline and in his special field of study.

Expertness can be the source of great good in undergraduate teaching, or it can detract from teaching, depending upon the values and interests of the professor and the manner in which he uses his expertise. We yield to none in our conviction that profound knowledge in a field of learning, coupled with the capacity for creative exploration and expression in that field, can contribute centrally to the finest teaching. The teacher who brings these attributes to the undergraduate classroom in the right way not only informs; he equips his students to learn with full effectiveness at the next higher level. The extent to which he does so depends in some measure upon elusive qualities of intellect and personality. Even college freshmen, however, are capable of sensing genuine worth and of thrusting aside extraneous factors for the purpose of learning better how to learn.

But the influence of great knowledge and creative capacity in the undergraduate class can be diminished in more than one way. It will be lessened obviously if the professor downgrades or neglects his teaching for the sake of other things for which his expertness qualifies him: research, writing, consultation, frequent service away from the campus, and related activities. The extent to which these things do injury varies, of course, from field to field and likewise from person to person. As we have indicated earlier in this memorandum, the neglect or downgrading need not be a consequence. On the contrary, research, writing, consultation at home or abroad can lend new dimensions of motivation and effectiveness to teaching.

As we have also suggested, the professor, whatever the level of his expertness, can dissipate his teaching effectiveness by the manner in which he approaches his students. When he views his teaching task as that of "laying out" his subject, when he sees his role as that of consciously benefiting a student audience, the benefits of his expertness are diminished, regardless of student capacity to separate the gold from the dross. Such is human weakness that some teachers cherish, consciously or subconsciously, the authority over students which is bequeathed upon them in the classroom. They treasure grading as an arm of that authority. They avoid endangering their prestige as experts by any sharing of learning that might equip students to challenge their authority. Fortunately, such extreme pettiness is infrequent. Hopefully, it is a phenomenon that appears even less frequently among beginning undergraduate teachers.

Sharing with learners

Fine teaching will happen when the expert, or better, the learned or artistically competent man, approaches his students in the spirit of one thinking or one creating, to paraphrase Whitehead. It will happen when the teacher achieves, without artificiality, the spirit of learning as an enterprise shared between senior and junior colleague. It will happen when the professor carries forward his research or the development of his artistic concepts before his student public in such a way as gradually to be able to benefit from the participation of that public in his own labors.

Admittedly, this approach to teaching has about it something of the ideal. Yet it has been practiced by some of the greatest of college and university professors. It is a demonstrably effective way to bridge the commonly perceived canyon between teaching and research, with reciprocal benefits to each. It is offered as a norm or model for the beginning undergraduate teacher. To the extent that he and his students can see their common task as that of bringing the resources of a discipline to bear upon important and unsolved problems, all will be conscious of learning as a shared undertaking. In saying this we do not intend to shrug off the most elementary and inescapable parts of the professor's job. The basic learning, the long hours of preparation, the tedious but unavoidable paper work in all teaching, the difficult evaluation of student performance; all of these must be acknowledged and respected. But they must also be put into the context of the shared learning which is their consummation.

Perhaps the concept of shared learning should be more concretely illustrated. Let us suppose that an English professor has become interested in the possibility that Shakespeare's *Henry the Eighth* was in fact written by someone else. If this professor wished to play the role of undisputed expert, he might overwhelm his students with his evidence and subsequently obtain bluebook reiterations, often garbled and incomplete, of what he has said, although this kind of uncritical response is occurring with less frequency in this generation of students. Or the professor could ignore both the play and his own theory, thus keeping his classroom and his study quite separate. On the other hand, he might decide that his class, even an elementary class, could provide a laboratory for the testing of his hypothesis. In doing so, he must be at some pains to prevent his students becoming premature converts by pointing the way to writings supportive of Shakespeare's authorship. He will want to sensitize them to stylistic analysis so that they can initiate their own direct comparisons, even though he may know that only the ablest students can make noticeable progress on this front. He will surely raise the question of ideational congruities between this play and others certainly by Shakespeare. It is then by no means unlikely that a point or two will emerge from the apprentice critics in support or refutation of his thesis. It may be taken as certain that the teacher, having successfully armed his own junior critics, will be forced into a deeper consideration of the subject as he defends his hypothesis. When this happens, there can be no question of the irrelevance of research to teaching or of interference of research with teaching.

Admittedly the example is a simplified one, and one must of course ask whether this approach to teaching is feasible in other fields. Within the humanities there appears to be no question. Outside them, the problem may be harder, although it takes no great amount of imagination to think of possibilities in sociology, economics, political science, psychology, anthropology, and geography. Perhaps the greater the extent to which a subject seems to require a particular order of learning, as in mathematics, the likelier some students are to let themselves be scared off, believing there is no room for considerations of value, for aesthetic judgments, and for basic issues on which novices can speak up. Under any circumstances and in any field, however, these foundations are necessary to the development of those advanced students who will carry on, both now and in the future, the essential disciplines.

To recapitulate, we are not advocating a teacher who teaches only a set of skills. The beginning undergraduate teacher will more quickly and more readily attain the role of the senior scholar sharing the satisfactions of intellectual discovery with his junior "partners" if he begins by viewing his class as a group of persons between 18 and 22 years of age, with varied abilities and interests. His task is to establish a relationship with them whereby in three or four months they will have acquired not only a certain amount of knowledge, but also certain skills and interests. During those months, he must draw himself into their inquiry, and them into his. Out of this relationship must grow within the students a sense of intellectual or aesthetic challenge. Out of it must emerge a desire to continue the study of the subject or the discipline. One must applaud the young teacher who enters his undergraduate class with a determination to emerge from the quarter or semester with as many continuing and independent learners as possible. And one must also applaud the young teacher who comes from an encounter with his students feeling "I am the better historian (or whatever) for this."

Fostering independence

Let us consider in conclusion two other roles of the young undergraduate teacher. Whether he has sought to do so or not, he exerts a moral influence upon his students. This is especially true today, and perhaps most especially of the young professor, not far removed from the age group of his students. In ways he may not wholly perceive, the young teacher influences the feelings, attitudes, and values of his students, probably less because of his words than of what the students observe him to feel and be. They are quick to recognize the young teacher who is as much interested in them as in his subject. In him they find a bridge to relevance between the intellectual enterprise of the class or seminar, and the world beyond the classroom, beyond the campus.

This relationship between teacher and student can be intense and deeply satisfying without being personal in any usual sense. What some students want and need is to relate to a unique human being, one who has feelings and values and holds to a distinctive standpoint about the world. He is a person, not just a teacher-in-general or a mouthpiece for a discipline, no matter how learned he may be. What the student seeks is of the same essence as what Professor Carl L. Becker found gratifying in the intellectual relationship he established with Frederick Jackson Turner. It is akin to what another distinguished scholar once described as the sense of discipleship which the budding student develops toward the person and the mind of an outstanding professor, a discipleship which should be the first step toward ultimate maturity and mastery.

The reference to discipleship that gives way to mastery leads us to the consideration of one of the most difficult roles a teacher must play. It is the role which requires that he so teach as to make himself less and less important in the learning process. The teacher, as George Herbert Palmer said long ago, must be willing to be forgotten. His task is to help the student internalize the goals of his education and thus to free himself from any need for external motivation. It is to help the student sharpen the tools of his inquiry or of his creative effort so that he can proceed with ever greater independence. But teaching so conceived is by no means a self-negating effort. In the measure that he accomplishes these tasks, the great teacher becomes in the minds of his students one of the rare landmarks of intellectual and creative growth. And the student, in turn, is set more surely on the road toward continuous learning and toward some of the satisfactions of mastery itself when the wise teacher makes him a contributor to and not just a beneficiary of the teaching process. Whitehead puts it this way:

> The justification for a university is that it preserves the connection between knowledge and the zest of life, by uniting the young and the old in the imaginative consideration of learning. . . . A university which fails in this respect has no reason for existence. This atmosphere of excitement, arising from imaginative consideration, transforms knowledge. A fact is no longer a bare fact: it is invested with all its possibilities. It is no longer a burden on the memory: it is energizing as the poet of our dreams, and as the architect of our purposes.[18]

III   Teaching Procedures
and Strategies

One function of the young professor which merits extended attention is his role as a master of teaching procedures and strategies. This role, in combination with his role as scholar, is at the heart of his professional performance. What he does in the role will reflect the philosophy with which he approaches teaching and will also be influenced, of course, by the way in which he performs as exemplary and expert. The teaching procedures he employs are necessarily his own; they are shaped by his style. The selection of these procedures, however, offers a wide range of alternatives, among which the young teacher has considerable free choice if he will equip himself.

Course planning

The actual conduct of teaching is something done in the lecture hall, the class or seminar room, the laboratory, the field location; but it is also much more. It is the subtle, intimate meeting of minds in conference or counseling session, or in informal conversation. It is the fitting of educational means to ends on a larger scale through the curriculum, the individual course, the combination of the experiences offered the student, and the system of evaluation of student performance and development. In a measure that varies from institution to institution according to size and kind, the young professor will "teach" in each and all of these ways, and perhaps in others.

Curriculum revision has become almost a continuous way of life in many colleges and universities sensitive to the growth of knowledge and changing societal needs and responsive to the insistent requests of students and many faculty. The chances are, therefore, increased that the beginning undergraduate teacher will have some share in this important function. He will have opportunity, not merely to reshuffle courses as sometimes happens in presumed curriculum revision, but rather to consider with his colleagues what the results of undergraduate education should be and to devise a program for attaining them. Among other things, this will involve consideration of the scope of knowledge to be presented in four years, the sequence of presentation, the range of choice permitted to the student, the skills to be cultivated and the manner of fostering them. It will also involve consideration of attitudes and values which the student may achieve, among these the desire and capacity to work independently, and the intellectual curiosity to sustain that work. While helping to plan the curriculum, the young professor will also be engaged with his colleagues in setting scholarly norms for the institution, in fixing standards for disciplinary adequacy, in planning cross-disciplinary ventures. While doing these things, he will almost inevitably be responding to the current student quest for relevance. He will be able to view the curriculum as a means for enabling the student to relate what he learns of the human heritage to himself, and to his role in the world around him. Needless to say, curriculum building in these ways can be an exciting adventure.

The young professor will also have opportunity to plan at least one and probably more of the courses he teaches. He will do so most effectively when he is able to see his own course in the perspective of the total educational program of the college or university, even the total program of his department. He will also build a better course when he has achieved that awareness of what his students are, what they seek, and how they propose to attain their goals, of which we have spoken. Whether the beginning teacher is planning and teaching his own course or whether he is working with others on a staff course, he must meet the same criteria of effectiveness, the same questions as to content and method. In responding to those criteria and questions, he is able to exercise one of the most precious opportunities of the teacher, the freedom to choose among a wide range of alternatives.

The most important relationship a teacher must decide as he plans his course is that between ends and means, between what he proposes to accomplish in the course and the procedures he employs to attain his purposes. Before the relationship can be ascertained, of course, the young professor must first have thought through the course purposes. One wonders how often college teachers do sufficiently particularize, even for themselves, the ends they espouse. What kinds of knowledge do they want the students to gain? How organized? What skills? How are the knowledge and skills to be related to attitudes and values? What would the teachers have remain after the details are forgotten?

Having thought about the purposes of a course, the teacher must next determine what procedures are most likely to fulfill those purposes. To put the question in the language of the behavioral scientist, what do given results mean operationally; or, to put it another way, what steps specifically must be taken to bring about what changes in student intellectual and attitudinal behavior? For example, in what ways should the students experience inquiry or research? Until the young teacher answers these questions in a manner that becomes reflected in his teaching, there may be serious discrepancies between what he professes or believes is happening and what is actually taking place.

It is not uncommon for teachers, who think of themselves as aiming at the improvement of the problem-solving skills of their students, unconsciously to conduct their classes in such a way that they are mainly dispensing information. Sometimes a teacher, while professing his belief that students should grow in their ability to express themselves orally and learn, through the give and take of class discussion, some of the skills of reasonable and disciplined conversation, nevertheless defeats his purpose by his own inability to stop talking long enough to give the students a chance. The observation is not simply the familiar one of a discrepancy between preachment and practice, among all too human professors, but the assertion that educational purposes in particular too seldom get carried out systematically.

One may, of course, dispute the wisdom of any particular set of aims, no matter how carefully they may be specified in terms of changed student behavior. In fact, the vital teacher usually keeps questioning and modifying his aims, as situations and students change. To have formulated desirable outcomes, however, is a long step toward satisfying accomplishment. Not only is one able to choose means with ends clearly in mind, but possibly more important, he is able to change those means —in mid-course or in subsequent course—if they seem to be failing.

Let us examine some of the procedures that may be available to the beginning teacher and explore their relative advantages. As we do so it is important to recognize two things. The option among procedures may be less in staff courses, or even in courses assigned to beginning college teachers where the classes are large and the approaches somewhat weighted by tradition. Secondly, we must recognize the difficulty and the danger of generalizing about any procedure. As in any other human enterprise, the most effective way to do the job must be determined by pragmatic variation from general principles and previous experience.

Lectures

Teaching approach and class size are, of course, closely related, but the relationship is by no means a fixed one. There is a normal tendency in very large classes to use the lecture approach, probably in combination with some discussion each week in sections. It is also usual for the amount of lecturing to decrease and that of discussion to increase in proportion to the diminishing size of the classes. As the teaching groups shrink to seminar size or to the very few students manageable in the tutorial, lecturing is often completely replaced by discussion or even by the individual conference. Yet there are important exceptions to these generalizations. In both the universities and the colleges some professors choose to lecture even when the classes are of fifty or fewer students. In fact, the lecture is not infrequently carried into the small seminar on an informal basis.

Generalizations about the teaching approaches in given institutions must also be used with care. To be sure, there are many lecture courses with from 300 to 500 students in the larger universities. Within the same university, where the stigma of impersonality is engendered by the large lecture course, however, it may be true that much of the undergraduate teaching is done less formally in classes of fifty or fewer, possibly some of it by design in groups of seminar size, even in the freshman year.

Overall there tends to be in American institutions a prevalence of lecturing. And there is continuing controversy concerning the relative merits of lecture and discussion. Those who are dubious of the lecture as a teaching approach often cite Boswell's quotation from Dr. Johnson:

> Lectures were once useful; but now, when all can read, and books are so numerous, lectures are unnecessary. If your attention fails, and you miss part of the lecture, it is lost; you cannot go back as you do upon a book.[19]

This general attitude continues to prevail in England where lecturing has never been the favored teaching approach among either students or professors. It is not wholly unexpected that the Hale report on *University Teaching Methods* (1964) should conclude that: "Overindulgence in lectures should be classed as a drug addiction on the part of both giver and receiver." It is more notable that an able American critic, now chancellor of a large university, should state as strongly as he does:

> Using talented manpower as "talking books" is a shameful waste in most of our colleges and universities today, and tends to keep the student a permanent adolescent. The student's umbilical cord

must be severed at graduation in any event, and we should take the responsibility of playing midwife at an earlier stage.[20]

Without wishing to detract from the truth in these criticisms as they apply to much lecturing, we would redress the balance by emphasizing that both giving lectures and listening to them can be, and often has proved to be, both an active and a creative process, stimulating and freeing the minds of both lecturer and listener, rather than indenturing them in perpetual adolescence. Giving lectures and listening to them, moreover, continues to be a prevalent means of adult communication, amplified on both sides of the Atlantic by radio and television. Education in these arts would seem, therefore, to have a proper place in our colleges and universities.

In actual practice, there is not in any kind of institution of higher learning as sharp a polarization between lecturing and alternative methods of teaching as might be suggested by this discussion. Rather they tend to be used in some combination to augment one another. Research surveys and studies reported by McKeachie disclose a trend in preference, unfavorable to the lecture, however. They show that a majority of students as well as many professors have a strong preference for discussion, and many of these professors in fact practice it. The same research also shows, however, that the lecture and the discussion tend to accomplish different results. The lecture is the better vehicle for the transmission of information, whereas discussion can more readily yield the subtler goals of learning: the understanding of new concepts, deeper and more lasting motivation, greater capacity for change, for example. On the basis of his survey, McKeachie concludes:

> Other things being equal, small classes are probably more effective than large, discussion than lectures, and student-centered discussions more effective than instructor-centered discussions for goals of retention, application, problem solving, attitude change, and motivation for further learning.[21]

Lecturing varies along a continuum from formal to informal, the most formal consisting of the memorized address and the read paper, neither of which is common today. However, another kind of formal lecture, the highly organized, uninterrupted speech by the professor, usually from notes, continues to hold an important place in higher education, especially in large classes.

In the light of comments critical of the lecture, the young professor may wish to resolve in his mind two kinds of questions about this approach. He may ask whether what he proposes to say in the lecture is not covered adequately, or possibly better, in some combination of texts and other sources, including the rich variety of paper backs now available. He may conclude that he is, in fact, placing the information which the student can get from printed sources in a new context by means of his lecture, and thus lending perspective to the readings. Or if the lecture is in the field of his own scholarly concerns, he may find ample justification for it in the presentation of data and conclusions not elsewhere available.

Beyond this, the beginning lecturer may ask himself whether his students would be better served by a mimeographed copy of his speech, which most of them can read in less time than the delivery takes. The question becomes especially pertinent today when the formal lecturer has to compete not only with the mimeograph machine, but also with the tape recorder, brought to the lecture. He may still decide in favor of the oral lecture, recognizing that to put everything he has to say into a series of fully written manuscripts would be a formidable task, would deprive him of the opportunities for interpretation and interpolation which speaking from notes makes possible, and, moreover, would not serve the interests of his ear-minded students. He may recognize that the carefully prepared, well-delivered lecture can be a potent means of exemplification. And he may be aware that his own style of oral presentation, his flair for dramatization, can bring alive what he has to say.

Nearly everyone knows that an exciting speech may come off tame in written form. This suggests that a man's thought may become better than it is through his exceptional powers of presentation. The reverse may also be true. Irwin Edman has told of the somnolent quality of John Dewey's lectures, and their seeming lack of organization, an impression given the lie by a perusal of notes taken from the lecture, which revealed subtle but powerful arrangement of the points. Presumably these virtues would also have been discoverable in a transcription. Dewey's ponderous qualifications would have been there in either case.

McKeachie argues that the peculiar values of the lecture are seldom actualized. Yet nearly everyone has listened to lecturers who by their ability to emphasize points of importance, to pose searching questions and to organize complex material with clarity if not brilliance have made listening an active process in which the student is genuinely involved. Such a lecture may bring wholly new insights. It cannot only stimulate the student's reading, but also assist it. It can awaken interest and provide motivation.

When lecturing is done in this manner, it tends to approach the informal end of the lecture continuum. The informal lecture that combines in varying measure speaking and discussion is, in fact, much more common than the formal. Some informal lecturers are very skillful in presenting the "unfinished" lecture that leaves many questions showing. Some interrupt the lecture to make explicit the question with which they are wrestling and to invite or provoke comment. In some lectures it is understood that students may interrupt with questions or comments, and that the professor's presentation will be liberally interspersed with discussion. The advantages of informality flow mainly from the more overtly active role of the students, and from the change of pace possible for the professor. The possible disadvantage is the lesser degree of organization that can result from student participation, something which the skillful teacher cannot only keep in bounds but can even use as a stimulus to thought.

Discussion

There is clearly no sharp line between informal lecturing and the class conducted entirely on a discussion basis. In either case, the size of the class will be a conditioning factor with which the teacher must cope. In the very large group, significant discussion is hard to achieve, if for no other reason than the difficulties of real communication. In such situations, the division of the large group for discussion purposes is a device often resorted to. As has been suggested where the lecture prevails, one frequently used procedure is to break the very large class into sections for discussions once or twice a week under the leadership of teaching assistants. Another device for obtaining more discussion in a large group is to entrust a portion of the class, from time to time, to more advanced students, or even to a pair of students from the class itself provided, of course, another room is available. Sometimes a large lecture hall will permit groupings of ten to twelve students in—if the name can be forgiven—"buzz sessions" assigned the responsibility of reporting questions or comments back to the meeting as a whole. Another, somewhat unusual system has been employed with success: the professor designates, in advance or at the time, some twenty-five students as his discussants and proceeds to carry on the discussion with that group, everyone else acting as eavesdroppers, perhaps with instructions about what to note or watch for as the discussion proceeds.

Many a professor has said, "I prefer discussion to lecture, but what are you going to do with forty (sixty, seventy-five, one hundred) students?" With classes of more than fifty, some combination of lecture and discussion may be both unavoidable and desirable. When the groups are under fifty, however, one may very well ask of the professor: "Are you sure you cannot hold a discussion with a class of that size?" It will be more difficult than with a group of twenty-five, and it may be impossible to involve every student, but many a teacher conducts a lively discussion with classes of forty to fifty and gets at least two-thirds active participation. Moreover, the teacher frequently discovers that even the students not directly involved have profited at least as much, if not more, from the give and take of discussion than they would have from the most informal mode of lecturing.

The conduct of an effective discussion requires careful planning and a high order of skill in leading the discussants. These requisites are important because the discussion, if successful, frequently becomes so student-centered, as compared with the informal lecture, that the professor will talk much less than the class members. Although some professors are made uneasy by any procedure that seems to diminish their expertness before the class, some of the most effective discussion leaders like to confine their participation principally to the asking of questions, the sorting out of the answers that are elicited, and the posing of new questions that have emerged.

Many professors have difficulty in establishing their roles as discussion leaders because they have never had opportunity to participate in an expertly handled discussion, and so have no model ready at hand. In consequence, they tend to commit common errors that reduce the usefulness of discussion. Pace learned, for example, from university and liberal arts college students alike that lively discussions were rare in their experience.[22]

The leading of discussion differs in actual practice according to how tightly the reins are held, or—to put it another way—according to how narrowly or widely "relevance" is interpreted. At one extreme, everything goes: free association, sudden changes of subject, personal reminiscence, and other permissive practices. At the opposite extreme, a strong attempt is made to get the group to arrive at positions decided upon by the teacher in advance. Neither of these extremes can be called a genuine discussion. The former more nearly resembles a "bull session," while the latter is a disguised lecture or recitation. Good discussion, by contrast, is purposeful but involves much student initiative and creative interaction between students and professor.

Most experienced teachers would agree that discussion is not normally an economic way of presenting facts and that this cannot be its highest purpose, as McKeachie's studies have suggested. Rather there is good evidence that it can be a powerful means for inducing thoughtfulness about problems to which neither the teacher nor anyone else may have satisfactory answers. It can, that is, if the teacher, employing the Socratic approach, involves the students in the common task of exploration.

Other procedures

The seminar, which in recent years many institutions have shown to be a workable type of course, even at the freshman level, needs little explanation to the beginning undergraduate teacher who has usually had ample seminar experience.[23] If he is in the sciences, he has similarly had ample experience with laboratory teaching. Both the seminar and the laboratory can gain greatly in effectiveness if—or to the extent that—the teacher brings in his own research. Many an established scholar has testified that the best teaching he ever knew was when he was allowed to share in his own teacher's specific research.[24]

The basic principle for the seminar, as for the laboratory, is that it is not a way for the teacher to get out of work. Careful preparation can make the laboratory exercises bear freshly on the difficulties and rewards being experienced in the course. In the first meetings of a seminar, by informal lectures or group discussion the teacher can astutely lay the groundwork for stimulating consideration of the several student papers as they are successively completed and presented. If he fails to do so, he may justify the frequent saying among students that seminars are a waste of time, except for what goes into writing one's own paper.

The beginning undergraduate teacher will undoubtedly remember also that the value of the seminar or laboratory depends in addition upon the care with which the teacher counsels the student during the preparation of the paper or performance of the exercise and the thoroughness with which he evaluates what is done.

Tutorials may be thought of as small seminars which allow for a more intensive analysis and evaluation of student papers. They are probably more effective in an informal setting with from three to six students. One-to-one tutorials can produce superb results. They may be impractical and uneconomic in large institutions, and they are always dependent for best results upon a favorable match between tutor and tutee. Some professors, nevertheless, prefer this kind of opportunity for intimate work with the student. Under their tutelage, learning may be intense.

Consideration of the one-to-one tutorial brings us to the alternative of independent study. In general, independent study for merely filling out one's store of information, or for practicing insecure skills, is neither new nor on a par with learning under a good teacher. Yet the large number of laboratory guides on audiovisual film, and of other programed aids, now makes possible a form of independent study that relies both on such materials and on interdependence with colleague students, while the student himself takes the initiative in a new sense as learner.

The case method of teaching has a long and successful history in schools of law and schools of business administration. Some have argued recently that it may be employed to good advantage in many courses in the social and behavioral sciences and in other professional schools. Much depends, of course, upon the ingenuity and imagination that go into the construction of the cases. At their best, they can present an exceptionally strong challenge to the student to bring his theoretical knowledge to bear upon concrete problems. They cultivate judgment and the capacity for wise decision.

Experience has disclosed difficulties in the case method, however. Students frequently make two salutary discoveries during the early part of their study:

> One is that each of them sees something different in each case, and that this difference is due not to what is in the case but to what each of them brings to the case from his own background. The other is that trying to understand one another is more difficult than conducting monologues designed to catch the teacher's attention. . . .[25]

Another approach that calls upon the students to make decisions as a means of learning is the "simulation technique." In this approach, the student is confronted with a simulated problem closely resembling actual problems, past or present. He is asked to clarify the problem, assemble the data that bears upon it, and map out alternative strategies of solution, estimating the risks and probable outcomes of each. This technique, together with more structured game-playing, is being used with frequency in the field of international relations, sometimes with the aid of a computer. It aims to develop skills in the rendering of judgment and decision too often neglected in liberal arts education.

Yet another way to induce learning has been used and advocated by "group dynamics" psychologists. It is sensitivity training or the formation of "T-groups." The proponents of this approach make the point that truly meaningful learning emerges when students confront their own problems in a setting that permits and even encourages openness of social response. Consequently, when a class is organized as a "T (training) group," time will be spent identifying problems, acknowledging prejudices and other blocks to learning, and identifying feelings and attitudes to clear the way for more cognitive inquiry. Thus far, this technique has been employed mainly in courses in clinical psychology, social work, theology, and other fields centering around human relations. Its proponents advocate, however, wider experimentation.

We have very briefly described a number of alternative teaching approaches usable in the classroom. The inquiring undergraduate teacher will have no difficulty, however, in extending the discussion, either through consultation with his colleagues or by means of the selective bibliography appended to this report.

Before we leave the subject of classroom procedures, it is desirable to stress again one underlying requirement of any approach. This is the necessity for a sense of purpose that is clear to both the students and the professor. A clear sense of purpose is more important, indeed, than complete explicitness as to what the teacher expects from the students as their part in the attainment of these purposes in the common learning adventure. Most students will tolerate a fair amount of ambiguity on almost every academic subject except "What exactly do you expect of me?" The average class member insists on knowing explicitly what readings will be required and what will be the range of his optional reading, what laboratory experiments he must complete, how many papers he must write and of what character, what will be the nature of the examinations, and what will be the ingredients of his grade. The wise teacher will be judicious in meeting these demands for explicitness, so as to lead the student toward a greater measure of independence in his approach to learning. He will work toward the latter goal through his attitudes in class, in his counseling of individual students, which hopefully will be frequent, and in the actual formulation of the requirements of his course. Perhaps the most important thing the teacher can make explicit as the course proceeds is what he values in learning and how he will estimate with his students their progress toward those goals of value.

The wise teacher will also remind himself that the learning process, even in his own course, will by no means be confined to his classroom, laboratory, or office. If he teaches well, it will go forward in informal meetings of his students over coffee, in the residence halls, or on the bus. In some courses—urban sociology for example, or botany—the most significant learning may take place in the field, either on a formal trip, or through individual inquiry. Some part of the learning may take place at another institution, during a quarter or semester away, or simultaneously if the institution is near. And the teacher may also hope that the learning begun in his class will never cease, either with the final examination or at the boundaries of the campus. His professional concern may ignite sparks of motivation, and may even prove contagious.

Technological aids

Let us turn, for a moment, to the place in the learning process of teaching aids or "substitutes" for teaching, subjects of much controversy among faculty. We refer to all aspects of teaching technology from the simple device of the blackboard to such teaching media as flannel boards, slides, films, recordings, audio and video tapes, television, teaching machines and all the rest of the burgeoning battery of learning aids. Nowhere is faculty conservatism so manifest as in the stout refusal of many professors to believe that some or all of these devices have any relevance to their own teaching. This rather widespread belief requires critical scrutiny. On the side of the skeptical, Alan Cartter may be quoted:

> . . . however effective these technical improvements are for purely informational and routinized aspects of learning, they may be called diabolically illiberal. . . . Given the will and the desire, one can obtain knowledge from the book, the television screen, the magnetic tape, but wisdom, understanding, and tolerance—the essential aims of liberal learning—are attainable only through personal confrontation of teacher and student. Interest, individualism, and integrity cannot be mass-produced; they result from the personal interaction of man with man.[26]

On the other hand, the teaching of art history without a slide projector, of elementary foreign language without the facilities of the language laboratory, or of music appreciation without a phonograph is today almost inconceivable. Experience has demonstrated, moreover, that the televised or telephoned lecture is not limited to the mere transmission of information. Frequently they bring into intimate settings distinguished personalities who would not otherwise be available. As used at Stephens College and other colleges, the tele-lecture also permits discussion between the lecturer and the students. In some subjects the guest lecture being heard by telephone may be coordinated with locally projected slides or film strips. Or, by means of closed circuit television, a scientific demonstration, or a panel discussion, may be piped to fifty classrooms instead of being presented live but impersonally and less perceptibly in an auditorium. The advantages of intimate viewing through either motion picture or television have long since been recognized in medical education.

Many advocates of instructional television argue that it is no more sensible to consider this medium as simply a reproduction of a regular classroom presentation than it is to consider a motion picture film simply a photograph of a stage play. If television is to be employed for teaching, it is wasteful not to use the medium distinctively for presentations that would be difficult or unfeasible live, such as the showing of objects or events not otherwise available in the classroom that illustrate concepts under consideration.

The new media, mechanical though they are, provide the teacher with many resources with which to supplement his live teaching. The English or drama professor may wish to have his students compare the interpretations of Hamlet, by Olivier and Burton, on film. The biologist, of all undergraduate teachers, has perhaps had most experience in organizing lectures in terms of slides, to explain difficult phenomena clearly. The linguist is experienced in having his students hear on tape or record a variety of dialects. A teacher in almost any field may do well to seek out such experienced advice on how to improve the quality of conceptual learning by combining both visual and verbal presentations.

Furthermore, technological aids may permit an individualization of instruction that would otherwise be unfeasible. Thus, students may help to diagnose and remove their own deficiencies by having access to film strips, tapes, records, or information stored in a computer; and they may use teaching machines of one kind or another to facilitate drill on important factual material. Rather than dehumanizing teaching, some maintain, the teaching machine used under proper direction relieves the teacher of certain mechanical chores, such as the conducting of repetitive drills, and thus releases energies and time for those things which the live teacher can do better than any machine.

Some persons say that the time has come to transcend piecemeal reliance upon help from the media, and to program whole courses or even series of courses as systems wherein live instruction and a battery of technical aids are all carefully tied together in such a way as to maximize learning, even taking into account the well-established fact that students differ considerably with respect to the ways in which they learn.

Numerous evaluations of instructional television have shown both advantages and disadvantages as compared with live teaching. It is plain that at the college level televised teaching is generally inferior to live teaching, although there are certainly some situations where television is advantageous. There is furthermore some resistance among college students to televised teaching. Principally, students complain about the one-way communication, an objection that can be minimized by alternating televised programs with live discussion, or by such further technological sophistication as the provision of "feed-back" through radio, telephone, or even the pushing of buttons to indicate to the lecturer agreement or disagreement on various points.

Teachers will continue, of course, to differ in finding such mechanisms compatible or incompatible with their own teaching styles. It seems increasingly clear, however, that at least they should acquaint themselves with the resources of the modern audio-visual center before deciding whether or not to make use of its technology.

Aim of intellectual growth

The ultimate result of good teaching will be found, of course, in the student—in the growth of his knowledge, the extension of his skills, the lengthening of his perspectives, the shifts in his attitudes, the conscious re-examination of his values, the maturing of his intellectual or creative discipline. Does the professor give these sufficient attention as he performs the functions of measurement and counseling so integral to his teaching? It stands to reason that the closer he is to the student, in the tutorial or seminar, in the small class, the better is his opportunity to observe growth in its more subtle as well as obvious form. Yet even in these situations, many professors fail to gain adequate or accurate insight into what the student has accomplished, principally because they have not given sufficient thought to the goals of the course, or have not made themselves sensitive to changes that are not always disclosed in testing. Sometimes the tests the student takes do not measure what the professor himself has specified as the purposes of his teaching.

Tests and examinations are often, indeed, the most eloquent statement of what the professor values as learning. They fix the goals of the course, in the students' practical understanding. The construction of good tests, therefore, requires skill and experience fitted to the full purposes of the course, and these purposes must help decide whether those tests be "objective" or "essay" in form, whether the questions are given the student at the moment of writing or in advance of it, whether or not the examination is of the "open book" variety.

In large courses, and particularly in very large lecture courses, where testing is crucial because it may be the only means of measuring what the student has gained, the construction of adequate examinations becomes even more difficult and too often is given insufficient attention. And for this reason it fails, not merely as a measuring instrument, but as a means of teaching. The carefully thought-out examination, on the other hand, whether for large class or small, and no matter how difficult it may be, will evoke from the discerning student not only new insights, but also genuine satisfactions.

Evaluation is essentially for the purpose of estimating and stimulating growth, of disclosing where special help may be necessary, of revealing to the teacher where the intent of the course may have gone astray, what additional emphases are needed. Used in this way, it is both positive and creative. It can benefit the student as much as the teacher, provided only the latter finds time and occasion for some counseling.

The same observations apply, of course, to grading, which is simply a stated measure of evaluation. Grades may be used judiciously to spur learning. On the other hand, they are often used as a whip, as a means of placing students in categories, as ends in themselves. As a result, the student's first question too frequently is "What did you get in the course?" rather than "What did you get from the course?," or "What is your G.P.A.?" rather than "What have you learned this year?"

For this distortion of emphasis, we teachers must take some responsibility. But so must the admissions officers and committees of most colleges and universities, and those of the graduate schools. The habit of working for grades, acquired in high school or earlier by students aspiring to college, is sustained through the undergraduate years as an ever larger proportion of the students aspire to graduate school. When this happens, it is detrimental to genuine liberal learning.

Teaching styles

Beyond the teaching procedures, methods of learning, and media of learning we have considered, there are teaching styles. In the last analysis, teaching as well as learning must be individualized.

A person's peculiar teaching style is in large measure a function of his temperament and personality. Some teachers have a flair for vivid phrasing, while others are slow, painstaking, and analytic. Some are highly systematic, while others are impulsive and spontaneous. Some are lighthearted, while others are consistently serious. Some are almost always the same, in a large class or small, with beginners or sophisticates, early in the morning or late in the afternoon, while others are mercurial.

There have been great teachers who frightened, ridiculed, and badgered their students. There have been other great teachers, like William James, who were always gentle, kind, and considerate to their students.

There is, of course, no one right style in teaching, any more than in painting or writing, and therefore it is unfair and unrealistic to set for oneself or for another a model distant from what is consonant with one's own distinctive being. Yet there remains a vast difference between the teacher who has sought and found his own style or voice, perhaps after protracted experimentation and modification, and one who uncritically settles for the way he happens first to teach. Teaching is a personal but not a private act, and somehow the teacher's immediate public will provide him clues for indicated revisions of his performance. Only in the rare and fortunate instance will a teacher discover his mature style between the gaining of his last degree and the teaching of his first course.

It may be hoped that when a teacher has begun to discover the style most consonant with his own temperament, it will be a style that exemplifies to students the learner at work. In the fullness of years, Carl Jung said that he had never had a patient from whom he had not learned. One teaches best what it is like to be a learner by visibly and impressively being one.

IV   The Evaluation of One's Teaching

Despite the mixed reactions that the mention of teaching evaluation can produce in any college or university faculty, the fact remains that almost every teacher is being evaluated continuously. The young teacher cannot help being concerned to estimate his own success, and his self-evaluations are colored by his sense of others' evaluations. His students assess in every class what they regard as the effectiveness of his teaching and pass the word to other students. His faculty colleagues form judgments, usually from impressions or from hearsay. The department head and the dean, even the president in many institutions, is usually alert to what is being said about teaching performance, sometimes because they wish to assist the young teacher and more frequently because teaching is a component in future decisions to reappoint, promote, and offer tenure.

The question that must concern the young teacher is how discerning, thorough, accurate, and fair is this informal and non-systematic kind of evaluation by others that is nevertheless going to influence his career. His judgment on the question is likely to color his own behavior in relevant ways. The question is of greater urgency today, despite some of the trends in evaluation, because many students and some faculty are insistent upon and quite sophisticated about teaching of good quality.

Among faculty members

In most institutions, the beginning teacher feels the self-evaluation of his own teaching to be a lonely task. He may be helped by some discriminating comments from his students, either sought or volunteered; or he may obtain perspective on what he is doing in course preparation

56

or in class by comparing notes with other teachers and, with their permission, visiting their classes. In a slowly growing number of colleges and universities, he can obtain more systematic help through extended orientation or improvement seminars for beginning teachers, or through the availability of film or tape to assist him in self-evaluation. The number of such institutions is still small, however.

The present state of regularized evaluation is not generally encouraging. A comparison of surveys conducted by Dean John W. Gustad in 1961 and by the American Council on Education in 1966 shows almost no progress and some regression in the practice of evaluation, as a matter of good administration. The department head or dean today is the most important source of judgment in every category of institution sampled—universities, liberal arts colleges, teachers colleges, and junior colleges. This is perhaps sound, but its soundness depends upon the sources of information to which the dean or department head must turn. The opinion of colleagues continues to rank high, but both informal student opinions and systematic student ratings have lost ground as sources of information. The practice of committee evaluation has grown substantially, however. Classroom visits have dropped almost to the bottom of the list of sources of information in the universities and liberal arts colleges, though they are still much depended upon in junior colleges. Long-term follow-up of students has declined overall as a measure of teaching, student examination performance continues at about the midpoint in relative importance, whereas grade distribution has tended to rise or remain above the midpoint among criteria. Meanwhile, scholarly research and publication now appears near the top of the list as an index of teaching in every category of institution except the junior college. One can readily acknowledge that the depth, quality, and orderly nature of a teacher's knowledge can be measured in this manner, but not necessarily his capacity to plan or conduct his teaching, nor his impact upon students. Not more than a third of the colleges, universities, or schools within the universities report the use of rating forms, and in no category are more than 5% engaged in any research on better techniques for evaluating teaching.[27]

Can the evaluation of teaching be done more fairly, thoroughly and helpfully? There are no simple answers to this question. A Yale University *ad hoc* committee on policies and procedures for tenure appointments reported in 1965 its strong belief that evaluation to help improve teaching should be sharply distinguished from evaluation to assist in appointments or promotion. The committee concluded that, "The problem of evaluating teaching is one for which no solution seems altogether satisfactory."[28]

Out of limited experience in the preparation of undergraduate teachers and from recent research and thought on the subject, there have emerged nevertheless some useful patterns and models.

The first step toward helpful evaluation is to establish between the beginning teacher and his new colleagues an explicit understanding of what is to be valued and evaluated, and a habit of continuing communication. This can be begun in a number of ways. Not least of them is the frank discussion of what will be expected of the teacher when new faculty members are sought, or early conferences between the arriving teacher and the dean, department head, or a designated member of the faculty with considerable and successful teaching experience. Many institutions approach some or all of the task in more formal fashion. A large proportion of them (more at the junior college and state college levels than at others) hold pre-registration orientation sessions for newly hired faculty. About one third of all institutions and about a seventh of the departments in these institutions conduct seminars for new college teachers. A very small proportion offer summer institutes, and in about a fourth overall the new teacher is associated with a designated member of the faculty for continuing supervision.[29]

When it is done successfully, the kind of orientation and supervision suggested becomes a cooperative venture between the several new teachers and those who are conducting the orientation. And it relates fundamentally, not superficially, to the whole spectrum of teaching functions: the planning of the course and the clear delineation of its purposes, the development of reasonable procedures for conducting the course in a manner that will attain its purposes. Among the teaching components to be considered are the readings, the laboratory program, the activities away from campus when these are involved, classroom approaches and procedures, and the kinds of student evaluation and counseling that may be most effective.

Various methods have been used, also, to help the beginning teacher realize in his teaching those things that are valued and have been made clear to him. One approach is that of the continuing seminar, normally under the direction of an experienced member of the faculty, in which the young faculty and teaching assistants have opportunity to discuss and evaluate each other's work. This approach is used at both Harvard and Yale, and at a number of other institutions, and has proved to be an excellent foundation for sustained self-evaluation. At Harvard, seminar members have listened to the tape-recorded lectures and discussions of unidentified members of the faculty and made them the subject of critical examination. In such an approach, the merits and demerits of various kinds and styles of lecturing quickly become obvious; good and bad elements in discussion leading may become painfully apparent, even though the leader of the recorded discussion may not have been conscious of them. One tape, for example, illustrated the not infrequent tendency of earnest teachers conducting discussion not to hear the comments of certain students, or to cut others off too quickly. After considerable exposure to the tapes of other professors, the teaching of the seminar members themselves can be recorded and made the subject of seminar discussion. Many a beginning teacher has discovered that he is making the same mistakes for which he has criticized the unidentified professors earlier in the seminar.

Video as well as audio tapes are being used with increasing frequency as means for the self-evaluation of teaching in college classes, and their use is not confined to beginning teachers. One of the most promising experiments in this direction is that at Stanford University which has been conducted by Dwight Allen and Robert N. Bush.

Another form of in-service training that can make evaluation more germane and more fair is the master-teacher approach in use at a number of colleges and universities. At Antioch, for example, Danforth teaching interns invite professors who have a reputation for distinguished teaching to demonstrate and discuss their methods in a seminar. At Harvard the young Ph.D. who is just beginning his teaching is paired with an established professor. In many smaller colleges, the process of counseling by experienced teachers frequently goes forward informally within departments.

Classroom visitation can be both a means toward teaching improvement and a helpful mode of evaluation. Such visitation, or the practice of the "open classroom," runs counter to current academic tradition, and has lost ground in recent years. Despite this trend, the device of visitation has much to recommend it, and the beginning teacher should consider inviting a friendly colleague to visit on days when things are likely to be interesting or go well. The "open classroom" assumes that teaching is a personal but not a private act. It further assumes that the direct observations of students—so often the sole witnesses of teaching, yet so often criticized as being inexpert—should be supplemented by the observations of mature teachers chosen for the task because they are expert both in counseling and in evaluating the beginning teacher.

With the best of intentions, self-delusion as to one's effectiveness as teacher is a very real possibility.

The usual reaction of the mature observer is to wish to help his younger colleague develop his teaching and to employ evaluation as a means to this end. Moreover, discussions of young professors' planning, classroom performance, and handling of students, though time-consuming and involving realistic costs, has often benefited the institution doubly because it has been mutually helpful to the observer and the observed. It is with this in mind that Wellesley and a number of other colleges require department chairmen and senior professors to visit the classrooms of their junior colleagues. Some departments do not limit the "open classroom" practice to beginning professors but make it possible for all colleagues to visit one another's classes, and if they wish, to pass along their observations. When classroom visits are relatively frequent, the tenseness and self-consciousness of the infrequent visit may tend to disappear. Alternatively, the young teacher can invite a friend from another institution; some small colleges like Earlham encourage this because a visit that is non-threatening often can be significantly more helpful.

In the last analysis, the test of good teaching is good learning. Sound evaluation should be based upon this assumption, and some operational measure of the relationship between teaching and learning should be used, whenever possible, to supplement other judgments. Paul E. Dressel has assessed the usefulness of several such means.[30] Among other measures, he appraises the correlation of course grades with student aptitude, the measuring of student retention after a delay to discover what elements in the learning endure, the assessment of what has been learned by evaluating the quality of work in later courses in a sequentially organized discipline, the observing of the number of majors that are attracted to a department, and the use of testing immediately before as well as after the course to determine progress toward the course objectives. In each of these means, he finds some value and some limitation, the latter being principally the difficulty or uncertainty of interpreting the findings.

Better than such general measures of learning may be evaluation of the specific things the teacher does to assist learning and the effectiveness with which he does them. These may include, for example, the teacher's making clear "the change which the course attempts to promote, the importance of these changes, and the need for them," or his "demonstration of the new reactions [sought] and guidance of the learner's efforts in trying to acquire them," or his "organizing work so that the sequential, cumulative aspect of it becomes apparent to the student."[31]

Ralph W. Tyler carries this approach a step further. He suggests some basic questions related to learning. Since learning tends to take place when previous responses have been shown to be unsatisfactory, how does the instructor make the unsatisfactoriness clear to the students? How does the instructor help the students to select new responses that are adequate? How does he help students to set standards for their performance and know when they have accomplished them?[32]

Many other examples could be given of the practical steps to assist learning which those who would improve their teaching might find it useful to evaluate or ask others to comment on. Not least among them are the kinds of tests the teacher employs to measure the student's advancement toward the goals of the course. Too frequently, the gap between goals and tests is great. Suppose a course in music for non-musicians, and assume that the professor's intent is to induce some judicious liking, some genuine appreciation of the music of the Baroque and Classical eras. Assume also real consonance between these ends and the teaching procedures used. If then the final examination consists, as it often does, almost entirely of dates, names, and other factual information, and bibliography, that examination is obviously wide of its mark. As Dean Gustad points out, "examinations can be on the mark, regardless of type. There are even practicable ways now available for assessing the student's ability to comprehend, to solve problems, to deal with novel issues."[33] An awareness of these possibilities, together with some inclination to use them wisely, might well be part of the evaluation of teaching.

We may have seemed in this discussion of evaluation preoccupied with techniques and mechanics. We hope, however, that they will be viewed only as means to an end. That end is intensely human. It is the judgment of how well a human being uses his knowledge and skills to induce and increase the learning of others. There are intangibles in both teaching and evaluation that do not lend themselves readily to measurement. They are things that must be sensed and felt and can quite easily be overestimated, underestimated, or otherwise misjudged. But judged they must be, with all the sensitivity and depth of perception that can be brought to bear. Only then will the intangible role of the teacher as exemplar be given its appropriate weight. Surely those department heads, deans, and presidents, who consistently build faculties of men and women who are both good scholars, and good teachers have the capacity to estimate the intangibles.

Student evaluations

Until now we have considered the evaluation of beginning teachers by themselves, their colleagues, or those administratively responsible for the teaching program. We live, however, in a period of increased student concern about teaching and of determination to make the student voice heard: to help other students select good courses and good teachers and avoid poor ones, to help teachers improve their teaching, and even to influence appointments. It is ironic, perhaps paradoxical, that while student concern is growing, there is less dependence by administrators today upon systematic student ratings in the overall evaluation of teachers than was true at the beginning of the decade. Greater reliance is placed upon informal student judgments, despite the fact that their use in evaluating teachers may violate the rules of scientific sampling and may be in many ways unreliable.[34]

Student evaluation, although at least forty years old, has acquired a new dimension in the present upsurge of student discontent and activism. Formerly student judgments about teaching were essentially a private matter between an instructor and his class and not infrequently were initiated by the instructor himself. Today they tend increasingly to be public, especially in the larger institutions, and to be initiated by students; by the college newspaper as at Yale, by a political group such as SLATE at Berkeley, or by the official student government. Some of the long established and seasoned student ratings, such as that of the University of Washington, have developed simple but reliable evaluative devices that correlate well with what the student believes he has derived from a given course. Other rating procedures by their statistical weaknesses justify the apprehension felt by many faculty. On this point, Laura Kent's observation is apropos:

> Judging from most of the rating forms which I looked at, I must conclude that too often there are good grounds for the faculty members' distrust of devices now used for student evaluations. But this is not to say that no evaluation should be attempted. If present instruments are poor, they must be improved. To accomplish this will require considerably more effort, careful thought, and courage to experiment and to follow through by doing research, than is presently being manifested by colleges.[35]

Nonetheless, some institutions have both endorsed and supported student evaluation, even for purposes of appointment and promotion.

What do students look for in teachers? The specifics vary, of course, from institution to institution, and there is a normal range of judgment among students themselves. Academic qualifications gain first consideration: mastery of subject matter and the capacity to interpret it clearly, intelligently, and in depth; skill and enthusiasm in lecturing; the capacity to evoke and sustain stimulating discussion. On the personal side, students tend to value warmth and friendliness, absence of sarcasm, and above all fairness. Thistlethwaite discovered in the extensive survey of National Merit Scholars in 1960 that they cherished in the teacher among other things, "modifying course to meet students' needs and interests," "taking a personal interest in students," and "treating students as colleagues." They identified teachers who did these things as those "who contributed most to their desire to learn."[36] Among the ten items evaluated in the University of Washington *Survey of Student Opinion on Teaching* are "gets me interested in the subject," "has increased my skill in thinking," "has motivated me to do my best work," "has given me new viewpoints or appreciations"—all of them measures of the teacher's ability to stimulate the student's mind, imagination, or creative talents.[37]

There is, of course, much faculty resistance to evaluation by students. Some of it springs from anxiety about getting low ratings, some from injustices done in the published critiques of courses and teachers, some from poor sampling techniques. A significant part of the resistance arises, however, from misunderstandings about the process. Thus, it is widely believed that students are apt to favor teachers who demand little and are easy graders, who put on a "show" in their classrooms, and who are sociable and gregarious without being either sound or profound. In fact, if the questionnaires are sensitively drawn, students turn out to be capable of making fine discriminations, praising a teacher for his personality but deploring the poor organization of his lectures, commending the material he offers though wishing it might be presented more interestingly, deploring superficiality and expressing satisfaction with the teacher who is notorious for making heavy demands on his students and holding to severe standards in his grading. Moreover, research casts doubt on the widespread belief that "C" students' ratings are less valid or less discriminatory than those of "A" students, and illustrates the non-superficial discernment which students are capable of bringing to evaluation.

One of the most common student complaints is about dullness, and a high value is placed upon the capacity to be interesting. This might suggest to the beginning instructor a careful analysis of the reaction of his classes. He may be stimulated to make fresh use of his central freedoms: to discriminate among the many possible central ideas of the course, to vary and combine teaching methods, to focus less or more on the gifted students or the less well prepared.

Another characteristic frequently commented on is the instructor's availability or unavailability. The teacher who prefers to flee at the sound of the bell may find, after experimenting with different times for his office hours, some announced arrangement that is most effective both for himself and for his students, giving him the advantage of honest and full reactions and them the opportunity for well-considered questions and personal interpretations.

It must not be concluded that student evaluations are always right or of even quality, either at any one institution or as among many. In some instances the sampling is bad, the questionnaire dubiously complicated, the responses lacking in either reliability or validity. They are sometimes skewed by the inclination of students to be overcritical, or on the contrary to feel that if they say something critical about a teacher, they must soften this by finding something good to say. It is encouraging to discover, however, that many student evaluating procedures have improved with age and have come to reflect more mature judgments.

Miss Kent reports that some of the better rating forms contain items which imply that "the student is involved in and at least partially responsible for the learning situation" and are not just passive recipients of learning. Thus the question "How well have you assumed your responsibility in the learning and progress of the class?" or the criterion "This course has stimulated me to careful and consistent preparation."[38]

Joint student-faculty involvement sometimes takes the form of requests to the professors to draw the descriptions of their courses that appear in the published evaluation. Some go farther. At the Harvard School of Education, student appraisals are sent to the instructors for comment. Then both students' and teachers' remarks are printed together in a booklet called *Student-Faculty Dialogue on Courses.* Typical of student comments is the statement:

> Sometimes the course may be over-determined by the current preoccupations of the instructor. That seemed to be the case this past fall, as we tortured our way for two months through the question of what problems will be problematic in social studies. From the student's standpoint the course becomes disorganized as it becomes more and more contingent on the instructor's latest weekend insights.[39]

Faculty responses have ranged from admissions that a number of their lectures were "loosely organized, rambling, and at times presuming backgrounds that the students did not have" to strong counter attacks on students' lack of imagination and intellectual maturity. There were other responses also. "One instructor defended his choice of a non-directive teaching strategy, a second explained his criteria for grading, and several others used this opportunity to justify their emphasis on particular subject content."

Given present trends, it must be presumed that student evaluation of teaching will grow in scope rather than diminish. One must hope that it will also become more uniformly good in quality. And it must be considered, of course, as only one factor in evaluation, even as one acknowledges that in the largest proportion of institutions the students are the only direct observers of what happens in the classroom. Sensitive to the long-run effects of teaching that escape direct observation, on the whole faculties react negatively to the use of student evaluations in any decisions on appointment and promotion, as has been made explicit by the Yale faculty committee and the Muscatine committee at Berkeley. On this point, Miss Kent feels that the tide of opinion is turning and that many professors and administrators have come to recognize that systematic student ratings may be a useful supplement to current methods. She cites, however, the important qualification of Dean Gustad:

> However reliable the instruments we use, and however responsible, perceptive, and honest the student raters, the value of student evaluations must remain uncertain until we know that the qualities they are asked to assess are indeed related to the ultimate goals of education. And all too frequently, educators are even uncertain about what those goals should be.[40]

Two principles

Finally, in appraising evaluation from the beginning teacher's standpoint, we must insist on two things. We must acknowledge that there is no single Platonic form of the "College Teacher," no single definition of "greatness" that will fit adequately all cases. Any assumption that there can be is both false and iniquitous. Styles vary, tastes vary, and judgments about "the teacher who changed my life" differ according to historical and institutional context, and the background of him who judges. After acknowledging these very human qualifications, however, we must promptly affirm that all is not relative, and that a careful statistical compilation of judgments—especially the thoughtful judgments of closely related colleagues—will indicate agreement on traits and procedures that distinguish relative success from relative failure.

Ultimately, the evaluation of faculty, like that of students, administrators, governing boards, perhaps even campus architects, must be justified by the extent to which it can help foster an increment of learning, greater excellence in performance. The evaluation of teaching is now in most cases crude and subjective. The question cannot be whether it will occur, but only how it can be more sensitively contrived and its result intelligently used. We can readily assume that the more the evaluation of teaching is developed in these ways, the more we shall value teaching.

V The Preparation for College Teaching

The intelligent and perceptive young undergraduate teacher will sense the complexity of the task he has undertaken. He will be aware of the intricate combination of knowledge, insights, and skills required in the classroom, if he is to succeed in arousing within his students a feeling of partnership in learning, and help them discover the importance and the relevance of what he is teaching. As his experience broadens and his perspective on teaching grows, he will become increasingly conscious of its professional dimensions and exactions. At this point, he may thank his stars that his graduate school prepared him to teach and that the college where he is employed has continued to assist his professional induction. Or he may wonder why this has not happened and why he is left to find his own way by trial and error and to learn by osmosis. He may begin to raise some questions, to have some ideas of his own about preparing to teach.

The overall picture

Preparation for teaching is afflicted by the same paradox that characterizes the evaluation of teaching, to which it is so closely related. Although more than 90% of all colleges and universities put teaching at the top of their criteria for promotion, salary and tenure, the proportion of them that do very much to prepare teachers or improve their teaching is much lower. Although a survey in 1964 revealed that "ninety-one leading universities—more than triple the number involved two decades ago—were currently offering courses on college teaching or other phases of higher education,"[41] and although a growing number of departments in leading universities are concerned to devise some sort of supervised internship for their graduate students, the number of institutions with organized programs of teacher preparation remains proportionately small. In a recent survey of graduate schools, fewer than half of those responding reported any substantial programs.[42] The undergraduate colleges have also been slow to recognize their responsibilities according to Max Wise, who concludes there is need to discuss "ways in which graduate schools and employing colleges can agree to share the responsibility for inducting the new teacher into the profession."[43]

The need for discussion relates not only to the low proportion of institutions that offer programs or assistance in teacher preparation, but even more perhaps to the content and quality of that preparation. In some universities and colleges the thinnest kind of orientation passes for teaching preparation. Sometimes even this is received only by those graduate students who serve as teaching assistants. With them the orientation is often little more than a curtsy toward familiarizing them with the most obvious obligations of the teaching assistant. What is needed instead, and what a few institutions and departments have found it possible to provide, is a program designed to help the young teacher toward a professional conception of how to go about his job, and to help him acquire the tools for doing so.

As has been suggested, an indispensable element in professional competence is mastery of one's own field. It scarcely need be said that mastery means more when it is broad rather than parochial, when it is dynamic and creative rather than purely informational and static. When the breadth is such as to enable the young teacher to illumine fields in the discipline other than his own specialty, even to carry the quality and depth of his intellectual or creative concern into courses that cross disciplines, his path as a teacher will be easier, and the relationships between his learning and his teaching will become clearer. Even then, he will have before him the absorbing task of developing his grasp of the handling of his subject in such respects as sequence and pacing, so as to bring out its full intellectual power and coherence.

The other central element in preparation for the profession of college teaching centers around the interaction between professor and student in the teaching process. This interaction is also complex, as complex as cellular biology, particle physics, logic, American literature, or musicology. It, too, demands mastery, not only at the theoretical and ideational levels, but also, because it is an applied art, in practice.

If the teacher is to stimulate undergraduates and to draw them with some measure of enthusiasm into a partnership of intellectual or creative

growth and discovery, he should, of course, have personal characteristics favorable to this outcome. He needs more than a native capacity
for understanding young men and women emerging from late adolescence, however; more than an instinctive conception of how to help
these students shape themselves as intelligent, civilized, concerned
young adults; more also than some set formula for helping them acquire
a professional competence in the fields he is teaching. Important as
these are, he will benefit in addition from some insight into the learning
abilities and processes of his students, some skilled capacity to adapt his
teaching to these and still obtain the results he seeks. Only thus, will he
begin to develop a style by means of which he can maximize his teaching potential.

To acquire such insights and the ability to use them in deepening
students' learning should not be a casual undertaking. On the contrary,
it deserves special study and sustained experimentation, preferably
under the guidance of some member of the faculty, preferably someone qualified to understand the learning processes of the young adult,
in a manner comparable to that which Jerome S. Bruner exhibits in his
analyses of the learning of children.[44] No matter what his field, the
beginning college teacher will probably achieve better results when he
has adapted to his own situation, at least the simple proposition that
education must be related to the patterns of growth, existing or potential, within his students. From this proposition, as valid at the college
level as with children, Bruner evolves some very stimulating observations about a theory of instruction. These observations, together with
other literature that bears upon the relation between learning and teaching, might well be a central subject for study and discussion as the
prospective college teacher prepares for his task, or as he improves his
skills on the job. This is a real possibility, of course, only when the
college or university or department takes seriously the task of helping
the young professor prepare to teach.

Some present programs

We cannot ignore the shortcomings of the majority of institutions that
do not make serious efforts to help prospective teachers prepare for
their elected profession. Nor can we overlook the opportunities for
preparation that have been wasted through neglect or misuse of the
teaching assistantship, though it is pertinent to repeat Bernard Berel-
son's observation that Ph.D. candidates spend a considerably greater
proportion of their time in teacher training (effective or ineffective) than

do prospective secondary school teachers. But it may be most helpful now to point out some of the better programs for teacher preparation with confidence that they will serve as both inspiration and models for programs at other institutions, as the growing urge to improve undergraduate education gains implementation. And we acknowledge with Max Wise that in a few universities teaching assistants feel that "their senior colleagues look upon them as important junior partners" and "most members of the regular departmental staff are interested in them as initiates into the teaching profession."[45]

A few universities have developed careful plans to combine with study for the Ph.D. parallel preparation for college teaching. As Wise points out, graduate students in these programs are usually assured financial aid over a four- or five-year period, thus relieving them of both financial worry and any interruption of their progress toward a degree and a teaching position. He goes on to describe the normal procedure:

> In most cases the Ph.D. candidate engages in part-time teaching over a period of two years. During his first year of teaching responsibility he works under the close supervision of a senior faculty member but has opportunity to lecture and to lead class discussions with help and supervision from his senior colleague. . . . In the best of these programs several members of the departmental faculties work closely with the teaching assistants. . . .[46]

Among the institutions offering such an approach is Harvard, which has instituted a five-year, financially supported, program leading to the doctorate. The candidates spend the first three years on study toward the Ph.D., the fourth year in teaching, and the concluding year at Harvard completing the dissertation.

With help from the Danforth Foundation, which extended grants to five universities to improve the initial experience of prospective college teachers, the History Department of Washington University, St. Louis, developed a four-year Ph.D. program with the following elements:

> 1. Toward the close of the first year of graduate study students visit discussion sections of history courses taught by members of the department. These brief visits are followed by discussion of problems in teaching that have been raised by the visits. In the summer following the first year of study, the students prepare for teaching assignments by spending full time in reading. Toward the close of the summer they meet with members of the history faculty in a two-day conference on teaching and graduate preparation.
>
> 2. During their second and third years the graduate students teach under supervision in two history courses. In addition to accepting considerable responsibility for the discussion sections of these courses, the graduate students lecture two to four times a year. In one course,

they also supervise honors theses and, in addition, assist in preparing the examinations offered in the courses.

3. All members of the History Department faculty participate in supervising the work of the teaching assistants.[47]

Where the special four- or five-year Ph.D. program has not been introduced, grants have facilitated the establishment of internships to help the graduate student or the young Ph.D. gain helpful teaching experience. At Yale, the faculty has taken responsibility for initiating the more promising graduate students into the art of teaching, is affording them "limited supervised teaching experience under the guidance of experienced faculty" and is making available to the student who wishes it "the wisdom of those who are wrestling with issues of higher education as teachers, researchers and administrators."[48]

Antioch College is offering a program of experimental internships to exceptionally promising young teachers who hold the Ph.D. (M.F.A. in the arts) or are in the dissertation stage and who have had prior teaching experience. They teach approximately half time under the supervision of senior faculty members and have opportunity for discussion, "not only of the problems which the intern faces in his courses but also of the more general problems facing American faculties."[49]

Graduate students in the School of International Studies at the University of Denver are required, as part of the Ph.D. program, to study some of the problems of teaching and actually to teach under supervision, often in neighboring colleges.

Certain science departments of major graduate schools have lately become concerned that they seldom or never provide teachers for four-year colleges. Having decided that this trend may indicate such emphasis upon research as almost to require their graduates to seek jobs in industry or in other research-oriented universities, some of them are seeking correctives. They have introduced a few courses and seminars directing attention to the problems of the undergraduate curriculum, including the vexing problem of "science for the non-scientists."

These few paragraphs suggest, at least, some of the better programs for initiating young scholars and artists into the profession of college teaching. They are clearly helpful and they mark an important advance. Not long hence, however, these programs may be looked back upon as the first tentative steps toward a much more thorough preparation for teaching. For the most part, the present programs consist of opportunities to observe excellent teaching, to teach under competent supervision, and to analyze critically, as in the Harvard seminars, a representative sample of good and bad teaching, including one's own.

Further needs

There is need in the programs of preparation for more: for both theoretical and practical analysis of curriculum and course construction; for explanation, analysis and evaluation of various classroom and seminar techniques; for consideration of teaching and learning styles and their relation to the conception of teaching and learning as arts; for study of the growth patterns of undergraduates and of the adaptation of education to them; for discussion of the nature of the college teaching profession, its diversities, the freedom and initiative it affords, the responsibilities and obligations it exacts. Other items might be added as we consider what should be present in a program leading toward entrance into the college teaching profession that would compare, for example, with programs of preparation for the medical profession. The analogy is sound because teaching and the practice of medicine are both applied arts behind which lie theory and knowledge, acquired skills and experience.

One topic deserves particular attention. When the beginning undergraduate teacher accepts his position, he enters upon the stage of academic involvement from which he will find it difficult to escape, but from which he probably will not even wish to escape as he begins to discern the influence he and his colleagues can and should exert to bring about the fulfillment of meaningful educational goals. At the beginning, he will probably not be a member of the faculty committee on educational policy, nor of that on tenure and promotion. Time and the manifestation of concern and capacity will take care of that, however. On the other hand, he may find himself, because of his youth, a member of one or more committees, regular or *ad hoc*, dealing with some aspect of the student's place in the academic community. He may even find himself working, relatively early in his career, with groups or committees concerned to improve the curriculum, even to improve the conditions for good teaching. This will happen more readily when he has been articulate in his concerns, has demonstrated influence with his colleagues, and has shown evidence of a clear sense of educational purpose—all of which could reflect his program of preparation.

The young professor, in short, assumes a potentially active and creative place as member of the college or university community the moment he begins to teach, and this should be foreseen. Given the measure of lively growth and change taking place today in our educational institutions, and given the quality of young faculty being brought to them, the chances are the young professor and his colleagues will seize the gauntlet and begin to exert their influence toward bringing about the conditions which they believe necessary for the growth of teaching, of scholarship, and the appropriate combination of these functions in professional advancement. The chances are that none of them will be so naive as not to recognize that growth and change in the academic community as in all communities finds its effective expression in the political process. Most beginning teachers will have been exposed to this process in their student days, and many will have developed a skillful capacity to work with it. Some will be sufficiently sophisticated to recognize, within the institution to which they have come, not only the lines of political force, but also the underlying strength and location of the community elements that seek change and those that resist it. And they may also be possessed of the experience and wisdom to estimate the accuracy and validity of the judgments on either side. What they should have received from their programs of preparation is an objectivity and a breadth of views about it all.

This reference to the young teacher's community role takes its rise from the significant part he can play in helping to improve teaching and the climate for teaching. This role, in all its parts, he will perform better when he has been helped in preceding years to become clear about his aspirations for himself as well as his aspirations for the institution he serves. When he achieves this clarity, a quality actually rare, he will not only become a more effective influence within his academic community, but he will begin to realize the freedom which is his to exert if he will.

VI   The Nurture of Good Teaching

Up to this point, we have been directing ourselves to the beginning teacher who, whether he likes it or not, has a role in the year-by-year renewal of his institution's commitment to teaching. We turn now to the president, dean, or other administrator, whose responsibility is more often both overstated and oversimplified.

Good teaching, like any thoughtful human act, is made easier and encouraged when the conditions and tools necessary for its nurture are provided. Faculties have a right to ask for these conditions and tools, and colleges and universities not only have some obligation to assure them, but will serve their self-interest in doing so. Most administrators are aware of this, but the task of determining how best to obtain the atmosphere and the implements conducive to good teaching can most effectively be accomplished by the joint efforts of faculty and administrators.

Proper setting and tools

Some of the requirements are purely physical. Although the size, shape, and furnishing of rooms are not, of themselves, determining, they do exert subtle influence upon learning. Excellent teaching can overcome the detracting effects of cavernous rooms or close and overcrowded ones, but the same quality of teaching will probably yield even greater results under better conditions. An office that is sufficiently spacious and attractive, with room for books and files, and above all with privacy and a modicum of comfort, will not only enhance the young professor's sense of well-being, but will invite students and provide a suitable setting for the mind-to-mind association that is so essential to learning.

Lounges where faculty can mingle easily and informally, among themselves and with their administrative colleagues, where students can come together easily, with one another or with faculty, are also desirable. Residence halls, houses as at Harvard and Yale and Princeton, coffee shops, book stores that are truly book stores, even sources of coffee convenient to offices and seminar rooms, and other physical though more than physical things, are part of the environment for learning. They are the conditions that keep learning human in scale and conducive to intellectual and creative comradeship.

It is scarcely necessary to enumerate the tools essential to teaching. They would include, of course, a library adequate for the undergraduate program of a given college or university, in accordance with standards agreed upon by the faculty, and the librarians. Libraries should be inviting and should operate on the principle that learning goes forward best when there are the fewest possible barriers between the student and the book, periodical, or manuscript. The same norms are desirable in laboratories. And there should, of course, be a sufficient complement of audio-visual equipment and of facilities in the class or seminar room for its use.

We do not mean to imply that the conditions for teaching should be luxurious. On the contrary, they should be sufficient only to support learning in optimum measure. Where that line should be drawn will naturally vary from institution to institution.

Atmosphere

There seems little reason why colleges and universities cannot provide today the material requirements for good teaching, given the levels of federal and state support, as well as private assistance, available to them. Much more important and much more elusive is an atmosphere conducive to good teaching, for atmosphere inheres in human beings, in their relationships with one another, in their patterns of expectation, in the satisfactions and other psychological rewards they derive from performing well as teachers. Morris Keeton has written of the "oxygen" of a good atmosphere for teaching, without which budding student curiosity and intellectual enthusiasm may be suffocated. Keeton goes on to say that the presence of this "oxygen" in the atmosphere gives to the teacher freedom to set his own professional goals and style within a concern for good performance of his functions in the college. Moreover, it may make the difference between a faculty member's moving or staying. In a highly oxygenated atmosphere, the able young teacher may remain, not because of the salary or other extrinsic advantages, but because of the students with whom he can work, the congenial atmosphere of mutual respect and encouragement, the availability of a stimulating company of colleagues, and the opportunity to experiment as normal part of professional practice and growth.

Even modest sums are worth setting aside to facilitate faculty research and travel, attendance at professional meetings, and reduction of onerous duties surrounding the real tasks of teaching. They can provide for part-time replacement during a term when the professor is under pressure to meet writing deadlines, to complete committee assignments or otherwise to fulfill his professional duties. Such sums have again and again paid remarkable dividends in generating the tangible and intangible satisfactions so necessary to a stimulating atmosphere. The effectiveness of such grants is enhanced when a committee of the faculty participates in establishing the criteria for their distribution, in sifting the applications of their colleagues, even in assisting the preparation of the application.

Still another factor that conduces to the nurture of the environment for good teaching is a reasonable teaching load. Regretfully, this is not present in a large number of our 2,200 colleges and universities. Whereas a maximum of three courses is compatible, in most cases, with sufficient opportunity to keep abreast of one's field and to complete some study, the commitment in many institutions exceeds this. Often five or more courses are required. In addition to teaching, the criterion of reasonableness should apply, of course, to the other academic demands upon the faculty members—committee memberships, public appearances, and similar matters.

In last analysis, however, the concrete things—teaching loads, support for faculty development, the quality of the library and other teaching essentials—are less important in providing an oxygenated atmosphere than are other things less easy to pinpoint. Interpersonal relations permeated by mutual respect, however great may be differences of opinion on specific issues, can be a decisive contributing factor. An "open academic community," in which freedom is preserved and in which ideas can move readily, across department and division boundaries, through the presumed barriers between students, faculty, administration, and governing board; where doors are open, where sweet temper can prevail in tough discussions of the most difficult issues, where all the channels of governance are kept open and human— this kind of community can invite and hold able young faculty.

Administrative leadership

It can hold them, that is, if academic quality is another governing attribute; and if the president or chancellor of the institution is the kind of person in whom a deep, almost instinctive appreciation of these values, is combined with the capacity for a leadership that reflects them.

The nature of administrative leadership and of the governing board's approach to its tasks are vitally important elements, but so are faculty leadership and participation in every aspect of the life of the academic community. So also is the role which students play. As Michigan State's Committee on Undergraduate Education puts it, a central point is that

> the student has enormous control over the quality of education he fashions for himself. . . . He must actively pursue (and by pursuing help to create) the best the University can offer . . . in such ways as to contribute to that atmosphere of high seriousness which cannot but reinforce the values for which the University and its faculty stand.[50]

Today's pressures therefore call for fresh approaches and experiments in administrative responsiveness to group initiatives by students. The participant in academic administration, however central or peripheral his role, cannot proceed realistically without an awareness of current student concerns and drives, as they relate to issues both on and beyond the campus, nor of their implications for decisions which he and his colleagues, both faculty and administrative, must take. He cannot avoid awareness of the changes in American society that have enabled the student generation to obtain and exert greater influence, both inside and outside the academic community, than was true of their recent predecessors. He will be conscious of this influence and will understand its values and problems in this period of somewhat confused and sometimes painful change. Without such understanding, he would be not only less useful as contributor to decisions on academic affairs generally, but also in particular less effective as promoter of good teaching.

The perceptive administrator will similarly give thought from time to time to the perspectives in which each teacher must view his teaching, his own department or school, his college or university, and the world of which all of these are a part. As young teachers discover, loyalty and commitment can be great virtues, and the parochialism which these sometimes breed can be a destructive vice. The parochialism that drives wedges between departments and schools can destroy the faculty rapport so essential both to the understanding of the common goals of the institution, and to the communicating of basic principles through specialized study. The parochialism that builds symbolic walls around campuses, limiting the interplay between college or university and the world beyond the campus, runs counter to the long-run trend which is creating greater interaction between higher education and the concerns, domestic and international, of our local and national communities. In doing so, it places additional inhibitions upon the potential for good teaching. The parochialism that breeds disrespect for the faculty member who leaves campus from time to time to give his talents and his expertness to tasks within the larger community is not only disruptive of the harmony of the academic community, but can limit the benefit students derive from the teaching of him who commutes between academia and the world of affairs. This benefit requires, of course, that the commuter recognize and apply the most fundamental condition of good teaching—the sharing of his broader knowledge and experience with his students as co-learners.

Finally, with respect to teacher preparation, administrators have a particular responsibility. Faculties, deans, and presidents can set both a tone and a pace by asking of their candidates for teaching positions (and of the graduate schools in which they are completing their degrees) that they bring at least minimal preparation to teach, "minimal" being construed to mean what is now available in the best programs. They can, in addition, follow the lead suggested by President John W. Atherton of Pitzer College by launching programs "which will involve the faculties of all departments in ongoing analysis, discussion, and research in the art and science of teaching."[51] Despite the rapidly growing body of research and writing on this subject, some of it excellent, the preparation of college teachers needs much more exploration, much more involvement of individual faculties, much more involvement and support from administrators. And finally, the effort to improve teacher preparation will benefit greatly from bringing the recently appointed members of the faculty into active participation in the discussion. Fresh from graduate school, they are often acutely aware of the strengths and weaknesses in their own preparation. They also tend to be sensitive to what the institutions that have employed them are doing or could do to help a teacher teach better. It is important that their voices be heard by administrators and senior faculty both in the schools where they were educated and in the colleges and universities where they are continuing their education as teachers.

It is not possible in this report to state, even if we knew, all the conditions that will nurture good teaching. Those of you who read these pages will undoubtedly compile your own lists of exceptions and additions. What is offered here is a distillation of some of the experience, experimentation, and research aimed in recent years at the improvement of teaching. Obviously more can be said, and positively more needs to be said, not only on how we can create good teaching, but more importantly on how to close the "credibility gap" between academia's professed valuation of teaching, and its performance. Performance has flagged, not in any failure to honor good teaching, but in more fundamental ways. It has been found wanting in its day-to-day regard for good teaching as a valuable and sophisticated art, an art for which there must be sophisticated preparation, and about which we still have much to learn. The deep concern of the new generations of undergraduate teachers can join with the seasoned resolve of administrators in closing that credibility gap, so as to vest good teaching, illumined by good scholarship, with the value it deserves.

VII　Ten Principal Ideas
of this Memorandum

1. The beginning teacher should acquaint himself with the teaching environment that prevails generally in higher education, and more specifically in the kinds of institutions or the individual institution to which he hopes to go. In doing so he will be aware of the great diversity that prevails in higher education, of the choices available to him, and the limits of choice. He may find challenge in the teeming land grant university, the small struggling college of Appalachia, the prestigious college or university, or the emergent community college with its vigorous grass roots. If he does well his job of inquiry, he will not be misled by appearances nor mesmerized by false hopes. He may find the intellectual companionship he desires, the respect for quality performance, the breadth of horizon he seeks, and the spirit of innovation or social commitment in places that carry neither high reputation nor prestigious name. He should weigh, of course, such matters as salary and emoluments, teaching loads, library and other teaching facilities. But he should also check the attitudes of the institution toward teaching, scholarship, and the relationship between the two; the quality of faculty, students, and administration; the goals and organization of the educational program; relations with other colleges and universities; and the relationships between the college or university and society. All of these elements will enter into the choices which are his to make, at least until the mid-1970's when the supply of teachers seems likely to catch up with the number of positions available.
2. Although the young teacher may discover, both in the university and in the college, that he must teach courses outside his principal

80

fields of interest, or share in the teaching of staff courses, there is nothing except the extent of his own boldness to prevent him from placing emphasis where his intellect dictates, from experimenting with teaching approaches, or, in brief, from pouring new wine into the old course bottles. Nor is he prevented from arguing his preferences concerning content, organization, readings, laboratory requirements, and other matters as the courses are reevaluated. At the same time, he will probably have opportunity to teach at least one course or seminar in his own field.

3. The young teacher normally brings to his work a desire to teach and to teach well. In an increasing number of institutions "performance" and "visibility" in scholarship will also be expected of him. If he is worth his intellectual salt, he himself will wish to grow in his discipline. Inevitably, therefore, he will live with some degree of tension between research and teaching. With imagination, he can find ways to combine the improvement of teaching with scholarly growth. He will probably discover that teaching is best accomplished in an atmosphere of research or of creative expression, and that creative work and inquiry can benefit, in turn, from teaching, especially when it is conceived as a collaborative enterprise between students and teacher. On the other hand, the beginning teacher may discover that both research and teaching suffer when he does not keep up with, and integrate into his thought, new developments related to, but not directly involved in his own research.

4. Teaching is a broad undertaking that may embrace everything from the planning of an entire educational program, through the preparation of a specific course, or the developing of teaching approaches in lecture hall, classroom and seminar, to individual counseling and the evaluation of learning. The whole undertaking becomes more meaningful when it is informed by some concept of how learning takes place and how the teacher can best awaken within the student a process of growth that will continue to develop.

5. Learning, far from being any passive transmission of culture, is an active process in which both teacher and student play roles, the teacher by intention a diminishing one. It involves the acquisition of knowledge, to be sure, but also such intellectual skills as the generation of hypotheses and their exploration, the extension of perspectives, the deepening of perceptions, the heightening of sensitivities, the release of creative impulses, and the rendering of judgments. It means the development of complicated intellectual

and creative capacities, hopefully motivated by some zest and enthusiasm. It means the emergence in each student of an individual style of learning which the discerning teacher can help to cultivate.

6. As he approaches his teaching, the young teacher will discover as others have before him, that teaching improves when he gives attention to some basic relationships with his students. It becomes more effective when it incorporates a sensitive awareness of the students' capacities, backgrounds, and expectations both about learning and about their teacher. Literature is available to assist the teacher in verifying his own perceptions on these matters. Teaching improves also when the teacher does not attempt to "lay out" a subject, even one in which he is particularly expert, but rather draws the students into a sense of mutual inquiry or creation. A third matter, whether he is conscious of it or not, is the teaching impact of his very appearance before the class. When he is there effectively as the scholar or artist at work, his example can have a strong influence upon the learning of his students.

7. A wide range of procedures is available to the beginning teacher as he forms his own style and teaching approaches. His choices may be somewhat limited by the size of his classes and the structure of the teaching program, but even with these limitations, he has much latitude for adaptation and experimentation, provided he has equipped himself to do these things. He will teach not only in the lecture hall, classroom, or laboratory, but also in formulating or modifying the course, and in every personal interchange with individual inquiring students. At whatever level and by whatever method his contribution to teaching will probably be better when he proceeds with a critical awareness of what combination of knowledge, skills, and outlooks he wants the students to gain, and of the alternative ways in which he may bring this about. He will find it useful to bring to bear all the knowledge he can gain about his students. He may wish to consider the role in his teaching of library resources, of the wide range of audio-visual facilities, and of the field trip. And he may discover that his examinations evaluating student performance can strengthen his teaching when done in a manner that emphasizes the full purposes of the course and serves as a further stimulus to growth. Out of some combination of these elements, the beginning teacher will forge his own style.

8. Young teachers tend to evaluate their own teaching continuously; at the same time, their performance is being evaluated by students,

faculty colleagues, and administrative officers. Whoever is doing the evaluating, and whether the purpose is to assist the teacher's growth, to decide upon retention, promotion, or tenure, or to steer students toward or away from his classes, the factors used in judging and their validity and reliability are of utmost importance to the teacher himself. Some beginning teachers learn to use the evaluations of their students very effectively as a means to improvement. Some discover ways to gain considerable assistance from discerning colleagues. Some few institutions encourage classroom visitation and counseling by experienced teachers to assist the young teacher. And some provide seminars with the use of audio and video tapes, to aid the developing teacher. In general, there has been retrogression in recent years in the norms and procedures of systematic evaluation. Even so, the beginning teacher who is receptive can gain much help toward improvement from the results of evaluation. He may even exert his influence to improve the system of evaluation.

9. It is the fortunate young teacher who has had substantial preparation for the complicated and responsible task he is undertaking. Although more universities are giving attention to the development of undergraduate teachers, the nature of such preparation varies widely and the average is thin. In the best programs now available, the beginning teacher has opportunity to observe excellent teaching, to teach under supervision, and to benefit from the analysis and discussion of good and bad teaching, including his own. There is need for more: theoretical and practical analysis of curriculum and course construction, evaluation of classroom, seminar, and laboratory techniques, consideration of the development of teaching styles, and other professional matters of equal importance. There is a long distance to be covered before the preparation for undergraduate teaching can be compared with preparation for the practice of medicine or law. In covering that distance, the experience and views of the young teachers, fresh from graduate school, can be of great benefit. It is important that their views be heard.

10. The young teacher has a right to expect the facilities, equipment and amenities conducive to good teaching, although these need not be extravagant. Most of us need to be reminded that some excellent teaching has been done under relatively primitive conditions. More important than material things are the intangible relationships among the human beings that constitute the learning and teaching community. An "open academic community" in which

ideas can move readily, where barriers are easily crossed between students, faculty, administration, and governing board, can tempt and hold able young faculty. It can, that is, if academic quality is cherished, if there are open avenues through which the beginning teacher can find his way into a close working relationship with his colleagues. It can if there is adequate appreciation of the forces impinging upon higher education today, not least of which is the greater interdependence between the college or university and the broader community, and if there is opportunity for the teacher to move back and forth between them as he may need to. These conditions can be nourished by a discerning president or chancellor. They can also be cultivated by the young teacher, both within his own academic life and within the academic community as he gains influence. When he does these things, the beginning teacher will be serving the elevation of undergraduate teaching as a valued and needed art, and he will experience the rewarding satisfaction of helping fine scholarship and fine teaching to complement and strengthen one another.

NOTES

[1] Erikson, Erik, *Insight and Responsibility* (London: Faber & Faber, 1966), p. 131

[2] Cartter, A. M., "University Teaching and Excellence," in *Improving College Teaching*, ed., C. B. T. Lee (Washington, D. C.: American Council on Education, 1967), p. 151

[3] "Report of the Subcommittee to Study Student Life," *Amherst Alumni News* (Winter 1965), p. 19

[4] Keeton, Morris, "Is There a Future for Our Alma Mater?" *Mills Quarterly* (August 1967), p. 11

[5] Wise, Max, "Who Teaches the Teachers?" in *Improving College Teaching*, pp. 77-80

[6] Cartter, "Future Faculty: Needs and Resources," in *Improving College Teaching*, p. 133

[7] Riesman, David, *Constraint and Variety in American Education* (New York: Doubleday Anchor, 1958), p. 5; Cartter, "Future Faculty: Needs and Resources," in *Improving College Teaching*, p. 150

[8] Wilson, Logan, *Fundamentals of Education*

[9] McKeachie, W. J., "Effective Teaching: The Relevance of the Curriculum," in *The College and the Student*, p. 190

[10] "Some evidence to support this proposition comes from the work of Donald Pelz, Frank Andrews, and Leo Meltzer of the University of Michigan Institute of Social Research." *Ibid.*, p. 190

[11] Bell, Daniel, *The Reforming of General Education* (New York: Columbia University Press, 1966), p. 8

[12] Keeton in *Mills Quarterly* (August 1967), p. 12

[13] Sanford, Nevitt, "The Developmental Status of the Entering Freshman," in *The American College* (New York: John Wiley & Sons, 1962), p. 253-82

[14] *Great Teachers*, ed., Houston Peterson (New Brunswick, N. J.: Rutgers University Press, 1946), pp. 233, 236

[15] Rothstein, A. M., "The Lecture and Learning," *AAUP Bulletin* (June 1966), p. 218

[16] Arrowsmith, William, "The Future of Teaching," in *Improving College Teaching*, p. 60

[17] Whitehead, A. N., *The Aims of Education* (New York: New Library, a Mentor Book, 1953), p. 48

[18] *Ibid.*, p. 97

[19] Hill, G. B., ed., *Boswell's Life of Johnson*, revised and enlarged edition by L. F. Powell (Oxford, 1934), Vol. IV, p. 92

[20] Cartter, in *Improving College Teaching*, p. 155

[21] McKeachie, "Research in Teaching: The Gap between Theory and Practice," in *Improving College Teaching*, p. 230

[22] Pace, C. R., "Perspectives on the Student and His College," in *The College and the Student*, eds., L. E. Dennis and J. F. Kauffman (Washington: American Council on Education, 1966), p. 84 and *passim*

[23] cf. Taylor, W. R., "The Wisconsin Laboratory Course in American History," *AHA Newsletter*, February 1968

[24] Merton, R. K., "The Matthew Effect in Science," *Science,* 159 (1968), pp. 60-1

[25] Andrews, K. R., *The Case Method of Teaching Human Relations and Administration* (Cambridge: Harvard University Press, 1953), p. 34

[26] Cartter, in *Improving College Teaching,* pp. 159-60

[27] Gustad, J. W., "Evaluation of Teaching Performances: Issues and Possibilities," in *Improving College Teaching,* pp. 270-71

[28] *Report to the Executive Committee of the Faculty of Arts and Sciences of the Ad Hoc Committee on Policies and Procedures on Tenure Appointments,* Yale University, 1965

[29] Astin, A. W., and Lee, C. B. T., "Current Practices in the Evaluation and Training of College Teachers," in *Improving College Teaching,* p. 306

[30] Dressel, P. E., "The Current Status of Research on College and University Teaching," *The Appraisal of Teaching in Large Universities* (Ann Arbor: University of Michigan Press, 1959), pp. 7 ff.

[31] Astin & Lee, in *Improving College Teaching,* p. 13

[32] Tyler, R. W., "The Evaluation of Teaching," in *Preparing College Teachers,* eds., A. D. Albright and J. E. Barrows (Lexington and Atlanta)

[33] Gustad, in *Improving College Teaching,* p. 279

[34] Kent, Laura, "Student Evaluation of Teaching," in *Improving College Teaching,* p. 319

[35] *Ibid.,* p. 328

[36] Thistlethwaite, D. L., *Recruitment and Retention of Talented College Students* (Nashville: Vanderbilt University, 1963)

[37] Kent, in *Improving College Teaching,* pp. 326-27

[38] *Ibid.,* p. 328

[39] *Student-Faculty Dialogue on Courses.* Harvard Graduate School of Education, September, 1966

[40] Kent, in *Improving College Teaching,* p. 343

[41] Eckert, R. E. and Neale, D. C., "Teachers and Teaching," in *Review of Educational Research,* XXXV, No. 4 (October 1965), citing Ewing and Stickler (1964)

[42] Armacost, Peter, and Howland, Diane, "Preparing the College Professor for Liberal Arts Teaching" (mimeographed), Association of American Colleges

[43] Wise, in *Improving College Teaching,* p. 78

[44] Bruner, J. S., *Toward a Theory of Instruction* (Cambridge: Harvard University Press, 1966)

[45] Wise, in *Improving College Teaching,* p. 82

[46] *Ibid.,* pp. 82-3

[47] *Ibid.,* p. 84

[48] Miller, J. P., "The Teaching Assistantship: Chore or Challenge?" *Ventures* (Magazine of the Yale Graduate School), Fall 1964, cited in *Improving College Teaching,* p. 83

[49] Wise, in *Improving College Teaching,* p. 86

[50] *Improving Undergraduate Education: The Report of the Committee on Undergraduate Education of Michigan State University* (East Lansing, 1967), p. 48-9

[51] Wise, in *Improving College Teaching,* p. 92

Selected Bibliography

Bell, Daniel, *The Reforming of General Education: The Columbia College Experience in Its National Setting* (New York: Columbia University Press, 1966)

Bruner, Jerome S., *Toward a Theory of Instruction* (Cambridge: Harvard University Press, 1966)

Education at Berkeley: Report of the Select Committee on Education. Berkeley, March 1966

Examining in Harvard College: A Collection of Essays by Members of the Harvard Faculty. Faculty of Arts and Sciences, Cambridge, November 1963

Goheen, Robert F., "The Teacher in the University," *School and Society*, April 2, 1966, pp. 177-79

Improving College Teaching, ed., Calvin B. T. Lee (Washington, D. C.: American Council on Education, 1967)

Improving Undergraduate Education: The Report of the Committee on Undergraduate Education, Michigan State University. East Lansing, 1967

Jencks, Christopher, "An Anti-academic Proposal," *The Educational Record,* Summer 1966, pp. 320-26

Raushenbush, Esther, *The Student and His Studies* (Middletown: Wesleyan University Press, 1964)

Stern, George C., "Characteristics of the Intellectual Climate in College Environments," *Harvard Educational Review*, Winter 1963

Wilson, Logan, ed., *Emerging Patterns in American Higher Education* (Washington, D. C.: American Council on Education, 1965)